The Dark Side of GenAI

Exploitation and Compromise of GenAI Systems and Capabilities

DR. IVAN DEL VALLE

Copyright © 2024 Ivan Del Valle

All rights reserved. No part of this book, "The Dark Side of GenAI - Exploitation and Compromise of GenAI Systems and Capabilities" may be reproduced, stored in a retrieval system, or transmitted in any form or by any means, electronic, mechanical, photocopying, recording, or otherwise, without the prior written permission of the copyright owner.

This book is protected under the copyright laws of the United States and other countries. Unauthorized reproduction or distribution of this book, or any portion of it, may result in severe civil and criminal penalties, and will be prosecuted to the maximum extent possible under the law.

The information contained in this book is provided for educational and informational purposes only and is not intended as advice. The author, Ivan Del Valle, makes no representations or warranties of any kind, express or implied, about the completeness, accuracy, reliability, suitability, or availability with respect to the book or the information, products, services, or related graphics contained in the book for any purpose. Any reliance you place on such information is strictly at your own risk.

The trademarks, service marks, logos, and other marks and indicia of origin appearing in this book are the property of their respective owners and are used for identification and reference purposes only. The use of these marks does not imply endorsement by the trademark owners.

Printed in the United States of America

ISBN: 979-8-332-36980-3

First Edition

DEDICATION

To my beloved wife, Ruth Elaine Sus Cruz,

This book is dedicated with all my heart. From the moment our paths crossed, I have seen through you, glimpsing the depths of your soul and the beauty that resides within. Your unwavering support and boundless love have been my guiding light, illuminating the way even in the darkest of times. It is through your strength and grace that I find my own courage to face the world, and for that, I am eternally grateful.

I breathe through you, as every breath I take is intertwined with the essence of your being. Your presence brings me peace, and your touch fills my heart with a warmth that words cannot fully capture. You are the air that sustains me, the vital force that keeps my spirit alive and thriving. In your arms, I find solace and comfort, and it is your love that nourishes my soul, giving me the strength to pursue my dreams and aspirations.

I live through you, my dearest, for you are the love of my life. Your smile, your laughter, and your unwavering belief in us inspire me to live each day to the fullest. Together, we have built a life filled with love, joy, and countless cherished memories. Your unwavering faith in me has been the foundation upon which I stand, and I am profoundly grateful for your presence in my life. You are my rock, my confidante, and my greatest treasure.

As we continue this incredible journey called life, I can't be prouder to have you by my side. Your love and companionship have made every step worthwhile, and I look forward to many more adventures together. Thank you for being my partner, my love, and my everything. This book is a testament to the depth of my love and appreciation for you, Ruth Elaine Sus Cruz, my heart and soul.

With all my love, always,

Ivan

CONTENTS

ACKNOWLEDGMENTS .... **IX**

1. INTRODUCTION **10**
    ABOUT THIS BOOK 10
    OVERVIEW OF GENAI 11
    HISTORICAL CONTEXT 13
    TECHNOLOGICAL ADVANCEMENTS 16
    CURRENT APPLICATIONS 18
    POTENTIAL FOR MISUSE 21

2. EXPLOITATION OF GENAI CAPABILITIES **24**
    IMPERSONATION 24
    APPROPRIATED LIKENESS 26
    SOCKPUPPETING 28
    NON-CONSENSUAL INTIMATE IMAGERY (NCII) 31
    CHILD SEXUAL ABUSE MATERIAL (CSAM) 33

3. FALSIFICATION AND INTELLECTUAL PROPERTY INFRINGEMENT **36**
    FALSIFICATION TACTICS 36
    INTELLECTUAL PROPERTY INFRINGEMENT 39
    COUNTERFEIT CONTENT 41
    LEGAL RAMIFICATIONS 43
    CASE STUDIES 45

4. SCALING, AMPLIFICATION, TARGETING, AND PERSONALIZATION **48**
    SCALING MISUSE TACTICS 48
    AMPLIFICATION STRATEGIES 50
    TARGETING TECHNIQUES 53
    PERSONALIZATION IN ATTACKS 55
    IMPACT ON SOCIETY 57

5. COMPROMISE OF GENAI SYSTEMS **60**
    ADVERSARIAL INPUTS 60
    PROMPT INJECTIONS 62
    JAILBREAKING 65
    MODEL DIVERSION 67
    MODEL EXTRACTION 69

6. STEGANOGRAPHY AND POISONING **73**

Steganography Techniques 73
　　Poisoning Attacks 76
　　Detection Methods 78
　　Case Studies 80
　　Impact Analysis 83

7. PRIVACY COMPROMISE AND DATA EXFILTRATION 86
　　Privacy Compromise Tactics 86
　　Data Exfiltration Methods 89
　　Preventative Measures 91
　　Regulatory Frameworks 93
　　Future Challenges 96

8. HUMAN LIKENESS MANIPULATION 99
　　Techniques of Manipulation 99
　　Real-World Examples 101
　　Ethical Implications 103
　　Psychological Impact 105
　　Mitigation Strategies 108

9. OPINION MANIPULATION AND DISINFORMATION 111
　　Strategies for Opinion Manipulation 111
　　Disinformation Campaigns 113
　　Case Studies 116
　　Impact on Public Discourse 118
　　Countermeasures 120

10. MONETIZATION AND SCAMS 124
　　Monetization Tactics 124
　　Types of Scams 127
　　Economic Impact 129
　　Detection and Prevention 132
　　Policy Recommendations 134

11. HARASSMENT AND MAXIMIZING REACH 137
　　Forms of Harassment 137
　　Techniques for Maximizing Reach 139
　　Impact on Victims 142
　　Legal Measures 144
　　Support Mechanisms 146

12. FAKE DIGITAL PERSONAS AND FALSIFIED MEDIA 149

CREATING FAKE PERSONAS 149
FALSIFIED MEDIA TYPES 151
DETECTION TECHNIQUES.. 154
CASE STUDIES 156
PREVENTATIVE MEASURES 159

13. ETHICAL AND SAFETY IMPLICATIONS 162

ETHICAL CONSIDERATIONS... 162
SAFETY CONCERNS 164
IMPACT ON SOCIETY 167
ROLE OF STAKEHOLDERS.. 169
FUTURE DIRECTIONS 171

14. MITIGATIONS AND INTERVENTIONS................................. 174

MITIGATION STRATEGIES 174
ROLE OF POLICY MAKERS 177
ROLE OF RESEARCHERS 179
ROLE OF TRUST AND SAFETY TEAMS.. 181
COLLABORATIVE EFFORTS 183

15. CONCLUSION AND FUTURE OUTLOOK 187

SUMMARY OF KEY POINTS 187
FUTURE TRENDS 189
CHALLENGES AHEAD 192
OPPORTUNITIES FOR POSITIVE USE... 194
FINAL THOUGHTS 196

ACKNOWLEDGMENTS

I would like to extend my deepest gratitude to the guardians of ethics, whose unwavering commitment to integrity and moral principles serves as the backbone of our society. In a world often fraught with complex challenges and difficult decisions, these individuals stand as beacons of truth and justice, ensuring that our actions align with our core values.

The critical role played by the guardians of ethics cannot be overstated. In every industry, from healthcare to technology, from education to business, their vigilance and integrity safeguard the well-being of society. They remind us that progress must not come at the expense of our humanity, and that true advancement is measured not only by innovation and success, but also by the compassion and fairness with which we treat one another.

At the heart of their mission is the protection of core values that define us as a society—honesty, respect, responsibility, and kindness. These values are the bedrock upon which trust is built, and it is through the tireless efforts of ethical guardians that we maintain this trust. They challenge us to reflect on our actions, to consider the broader impact of our choices, and to strive always to do what is right, even when it is difficult.

In acknowledging the guardians of ethics, we recognize the profound influence they have on our personal and collective lives. Their dedication to ethical principles fosters an environment where justice and fairness can thrive. We owe them a debt of gratitude for their relentless pursuit of what is just and good, and for their unwavering commitment to the principles that uphold the fabric of our society.

With respect and admiration,

Dr. Ivan Del Valle

1. Introduction

About this book

In the rapidly evolving landscape of artificial intelligence, Generative AI (GenAI) has emerged as a transformative force, capable of producing remarkably human-like text, images, and even complex problem-solving strategies. Its potential seems boundless, promising innovations across fields as diverse as healthcare, entertainment, education, and beyond. Yet, as with any powerful technology, there exists a shadowy underbelly—a dark side that warrants careful examination and vigilant oversight.

"The Dark Side of GenAI" delves into the less discussed, often overlooked facets of these advanced systems. While GenAI's capabilities have captivated the imagination of technologists and the broader public alike, the exploitation and compromise of these systems pose significant ethical, social, and security concerns. This book aims to shed light on the vulnerabilities and risks associated with GenAI, exploring how malicious actors can manipulate these systems for nefarious purposes, from spreading disinformation to creating deepfakes that undermine trust in media and personal relationships.

Further, this work examines the ethical dilemmas faced by developers and policymakers as they navigate the fine line between innovation and regulation. How can society harness the benefits of GenAI while mitigating its potential for abuse? What safeguards and frameworks are necessary to ensure that these systems are used responsibly and ethically? Through a blend of case studies, expert analyses, and thought-provoking discussions, "The Dark Side of GenAI" provides a comprehensive overview of the challenges and imperatives in managing the double-edged sword that is Generative AI.

As you turn these pages, prepare to confront the unsettling realities that accompany the marvels of GenAI, and consider the collective responsibility we bear in shaping the future of this powerful technology.

Overview of GenAI

Generative Artificial Intelligence (GenAI) represents a significant technological advancement, enabling machines to create content that closely resembles human-generated outputs. Unlike traditional AI systems that rely on pre-defined rules and datasets to perform tasks, GenAI leverages complex algorithms, particularly deep learning techniques, to produce novel and contextually relevant content. This capability spans a variety of domains, including text, images, music, and even video, making GenAI an exceptionally versatile tool in modern technology.

At the core of GenAI is the concept of neural networks, specifically Generative Adversarial Networks (GANs) and Variational Autoencoders (VAEs). GANs consist of two neural networks: a generator and a discriminator. The generator creates content, while the discriminator evaluates it against real data. Through iterative training, the generator progressively improves its output, creating content that becomes increasingly indistinguishable from human-made data. VAEs, on the other hand, encode input data into a latent space and then decode it to generate new content, ensuring the output remains coherent and contextually appropriate.

The applications of GenAI are vast and varied. In the field of natural language processing, models like OpenAI's GPT-3 can generate human-like text, undertaking tasks such as writing essays, answering questions, and even composing poetry. In the visual arts, GenAI can create images and artworks, sometimes indistinguishable from those made by human artists. Music composition, video game design, and even scientific research have seen the integration of GenAI to generate innovative outputs that push the boundaries of creativity and efficiency.

Despite its impressive capabilities, GenAI is not without its challenges and ethical concerns. One of the most pressing issues is the potential for misuse. The ability to generate realistic text and images can be exploited to create deepfakes, misleading information, and other forms of digital deception. This raises significant concerns about the authenticity of content and the potential for GenAI to be used in harmful ways.

Another critical issue is the bias inherent in the training data. GenAI systems learn from vast datasets, which often contain biases present in human society. Consequently, these biases can be reflected and even amplified in the generated outputs, leading to ethical dilemmas and perpetuating stereotypes. Addressing these biases requires careful consideration and ongoing efforts to ensure fairness and inclusivity in AI-generated content.

The impact of GenAI on employment and the job market also warrants attention. As GenAI systems become more capable, there is a growing concern about the displacement of human workers in various creative and analytical roles. While GenAI can augment human capabilities and drive innovation, it also poses the risk of reducing the demand for certain skill sets, necessitating a reevaluation of workforce development and education.

In the context of privacy, GenAI's ability to generate content based on personal data raises significant concerns. The use of personal information to train AI models can lead to privacy breaches and unauthorized exploitation of sensitive data. Ensuring robust data protection measures and ethical guidelines is essential to mitigate these risks.

Generative AI represents a double-edged sword, offering remarkable potential for innovation and creativity while also posing significant ethical and societal challenges. As the technology continues to evolve, it is imperative to navigate these complexities with a balanced approach, fostering responsible development and deployment of GenAI systems.

Historical Context

The evolution of generative artificial intelligence (GenAI) can be traced back to the early days of computing and artificial intelligence research. The foundational theories and technologies that underpin GenAI were developed over several decades, with significant milestones marking its progress. Understanding the historical context of GenAI provides insight into its current capabilities and the ethical dilemmas it presents.

In the 1950s and 1960s, the field of artificial intelligence began to take shape, driven by pioneers such as Alan Turing and John McCarthy. Turing's seminal paper, "Computing Machinery and Intelligence," introduced the concept of machines capable of intelligent behavior, laying the groundwork for future AI research. McCarthy, on the other hand, coined the term "artificial intelligence" and organized the Dartmouth Conference in 1956, which is often regarded as the birth of AI as a field of study.

The following decades saw the development of various AI techniques, including symbolic AI and expert systems. These early systems were rule-based and relied on human-encoded knowledge to perform specific tasks. While they achieved some success, their limitations became apparent as they struggled with complex, real-world problems.

The 1980s and 1990s marked a shift towards machine learning, a subfield of AI focused on developing algorithms that enable computers to learn from data. The advent of more powerful computers and the availability of large datasets facilitated the growth of machine learning. Neural networks, inspired by the structure and function of the human brain, gained popularity during this period. However, it wasn't until the early 2000s that neural networks, specifically deep learning, began to show significant promise.

Deep learning, characterized by multi-layered neural networks, revolutionized the field of AI. Researchers such as Geoffrey Hinton, Yann LeCun, and Yoshua Bengio made significant contributions to the development of deep learning algorithms. Their work demonstrated that deep neural networks could achieve remarkable performance in tasks such as image and speech recognition, leading to widespread adoption in various industries.

The rise of deep learning paved the way for the development of generative models, which are designed to generate new data samples similar to a given dataset. One of the most notable breakthroughs in this area was the introduction of Generative Adversarial Networks (GANs) by Ian Goodfellow and his colleagues in 2014. GANs consist of two neural networks, a generator and a discriminator, that compete against each other to produce realistic data samples. This innovative approach enabled the creation of highly realistic images, videos, and other forms of media.

The development of natural language processing (NLP) techniques also played a crucial role in the advancement of GenAI. Early NLP systems relied on rule-based approaches and statistical methods, but deep learning transformed the field by enabling the creation of more sophisticated language models. The introduction of transformer architectures, such as the one used in OpenAI's GPT-3, marked a significant milestone in NLP. These models demonstrated an unprecedented ability to generate coherent and contextually relevant text, further blurring the line between human and machine-generated content.

As GenAI technologies continue to evolve, they raise important ethical and societal questions. The ability to generate highly realistic and convincing content has profound implications for areas such as misinformation, copyright infringement, and privacy. Understanding the historical context of GenAI helps frame these challenges and highlights the need for responsible development and deployment of these powerful technologies.

Technological Advancements

Generative Artificial Intelligence (GenAI) has progressed at an unprecedented rate, driven by exponential advancements in computational power, sophisticated algorithms, and the availability of vast amounts of data. Central to these technological leaps are deep learning models, particularly Generative Adversarial Networks (GANs) and Variational Autoencoders (VAEs), which have revolutionized the way machines understand and generate data. These innovations have enabled machines to produce human-like text, realistic images, and even music, pushing the boundaries of what was once thought possible.

Deep learning models, such as GANs, consist of two neural networks: a generator and a discriminator. The generator creates data samples, while the discriminator evaluates them against real data. Through this adversarial process, the generator improves its ability to produce realistic outputs. This methodology has been instrumental in creating highly convincing fake images and videos, often referred to as deepfakes. These deepfakes have raised significant ethical and security concerns, as they can be used to manipulate public opinion, create false evidence, and jeopardize privacy.

Another critical development in GenAI is the transformer architecture, which has been pivotal in natural language processing (NLP). Models like OpenAI's GPT-3 and Google's BERT have set new benchmarks for language understanding and generation. These models are trained on diverse datasets, enabling them to generate coherent and contextually relevant text. However, the same capabilities that allow these models to assist in writing and customer service also pose risks. They can be exploited to generate misleading information, spam, and even malicious code, highlighting the dual-use nature of GenAI technologies.

The integration of GenAI with other emerging technologies has further amplified its potential and risks. For instance, combining GenAI with Internet of Things (IoT) devices allows for more intuitive and responsive smart environments. However, this also introduces new vulnerabilities, as malicious actors can exploit GenAI to manipulate IoT systems, leading to potential breaches in security and privacy.

Advancements in hardware, particularly the development of specialized AI chips, have also played a crucial role in accelerating GenAI research and applications. These chips, designed to handle the massive parallel processing requirements of deep learning models, have made it feasible to train and deploy complex AI systems more efficiently. This hardware evolution has democratized access to powerful AI tools, enabling smaller organizations and individual researchers to contribute to the field. However, it also means that potentially harmful GenAI applications are more accessible to those with malicious intent.

The availability of large datasets is another driving force behind the rapid progress in GenAI. Data is the lifeblood of AI, and the proliferation of digital information has provided ample training material for GenAI models. Nevertheless, the reliance on vast datasets raises concerns about data privacy and security. The use of personal data without consent, the potential for data breaches, and the ethical implications of data collection practices are critical issues that need addressing.

Regulatory frameworks and ethical guidelines have struggled to keep pace with these technological advancements. The rapid development and deployment of GenAI technologies often outstrip the ability of policymakers to implement effective regulations. This lag creates a landscape where the potential for misuse is high, and the mechanisms for accountability are still evolving.

While the technological advancements in GenAI hold immense promise for innovation and progress, they also bring to light significant challenges and risks. The dual-use nature of these technologies necessitates a balanced approach, ensuring that their benefits are harnessed while mitigating their potential for harm.

Current Applications

Generative Artificial Intelligence (GenAI) has found its way into various sectors, revolutionizing how tasks are performed and decisions are made. One of the most notable applications is in content creation. Companies leverage GenAI to produce written articles, marketing content, and even creative stories. The ability to generate human-like text has significantly reduced the time and effort required to create high-quality content, allowing businesses to focus on strategic activities. However, this application also raises concerns about the authenticity and originality of the generated content, as well as the potential for misinformation.

In the realm of healthcare, GenAI has shown promise in diagnosing diseases and personalizing treatment plans. By analyzing vast amounts of medical data, these systems can identify patterns and correlations that might be missed by human doctors. This capability can lead to earlier diagnosis and more effective treatments. However, the reliance on AI for critical medical decisions brings up ethical questions about accountability and the potential for errors that could have serious consequences for patients.

The financial industry is another area where GenAI is making significant strides. Algorithms are used to predict market trends, manage portfolios, and even execute trades autonomously. The speed and accuracy of these systems can lead to substantial financial gains. Nevertheless, the opacity of these algorithms poses risks, as their decision-making processes are often not fully understood even by their creators, leading to potential market manipulation and financial instability.

In customer service, chatbots powered by GenAI are becoming increasingly common. These systems can handle a wide range of inquiries, providing quick and efficient responses to customer queries. This not only improves customer satisfaction but also reduces the workload on human customer service representatives. However, the interaction with AI can sometimes lack the empathy and understanding that human agents provide, potentially leading to customer dissatisfaction in more complex or sensitive situations.

The entertainment industry is also benefiting from GenAI. From generating music and art to creating scripts and even entire virtual worlds, AI is pushing the boundaries of creativity. This has opened up new possibilities for artists and creators, allowing them to explore ideas that would have been impossible or too time-consuming to realize manually. Yet, this also leads to questions about the value of human creativity and the potential for AI-generated content to overshadow human-made works.

In education, personalized learning experiences are being developed with the help of GenAI. These systems can adapt to individual students' learning styles and paces, providing customized resources and feedback. This can enhance the learning experience and help students achieve better outcomes. However, the use of AI in education also raises concerns about data privacy and the potential for bias in the algorithms, which could disadvantage certain groups of students.

Law enforcement agencies are increasingly using GenAI for predictive policing, analyzing data to identify potential criminal activity before it occurs. This can help in the allocation of resources and in preventing crime. However, this application is fraught with ethical issues, including the potential for racial profiling and the infringement of civil liberties.

The agricultural sector is not left out, with GenAI being used to optimize crop yields and manage resources more efficiently. By analyzing data from various sources, these systems can provide farmers with insights on the best times to plant and harvest crops, as well as how to manage pests and diseases. While this can lead to more sustainable farming practices, there are concerns about the accessibility of these technologies to small-scale farmers and the potential for increased dependency on tech companies.

Each of these applications showcases the transformative potential of GenAI, but they also highlight the complexities and ethical dilemmas that come with its widespread adoption.

Potential for Misuse

Generative AI (GenAI) has demonstrated remarkable capabilities, from creating art and music to assisting in complex problem-solving. However, these advancements come with a significant caveat: the potential for misuse. This aspect poses a serious challenge that needs to be addressed by technologists, policymakers, and society at large.

One of the most alarming concerns is the creation and dissemination of deepfakes. These highly realistic but entirely fabricated videos and audio recordings can be used to impersonate individuals, manipulate public opinion, and spread misinformation. With the ability to generate convincing content, malicious actors can easily produce fake news, leading to widespread misinformation and erosion of trust in media sources. This, in turn, can destabilize societies and influence political outcomes.

Another area of concern is cybersecurity. GenAI can be leveraged to create sophisticated phishing attacks that are tailored to individual targets. By analyzing social media profiles and other publicly available data, AI can craft highly personalized and convincing phishing emails, making it more likely that recipients will fall for these scams. Furthermore, AI can be used to automate the process of discovering and exploiting software vulnerabilities, making cyber-attacks more efficient and harder to defend against.

The potential for misuse extends to the realm of privacy. GenAI can analyze vast amounts of data to infer sensitive information about individuals, even from seemingly innocuous sources. For instance, by examining patterns in social media activity, AI can deduce personal habits, preferences, and even mental health conditions. This kind of surveillance can be used by corporations for targeted advertising or by governments for more nefarious purposes, such as monitoring and controlling dissent.

In the financial sector, GenAI can be exploited for fraudulent activities. AI algorithms can be used to manipulate stock prices or execute trades based on insider information. Additionally, AI-generated synthetic identities can be used to commit various forms of financial fraud, such as opening bank accounts or applying for loans under false pretenses. These activities can undermine the integrity of financial systems and cause significant economic damage.

The ethical implications of GenAI's potential for misuse also raise important questions. Bias in AI models can perpetuate and even exacerbate existing social inequalities. For example, biased algorithms used in hiring processes can unfairly disadvantage certain groups, leading to discrimination and reduced opportunities for marginalized communities. Moreover, the use of AI in law enforcement and judicial systems can result in biased outcomes, eroding public trust in these institutions.

Addressing the potential for misuse requires a multi-faceted approach. Technological solutions, such as improved detection methods for deepfakes and more robust cybersecurity measures, are essential. Equally important are regulatory frameworks that set clear guidelines for the ethical use of AI. Public awareness and education can also play a crucial role in mitigating the risks associated with GenAI. By understanding the potential dangers, individuals and organizations can take proactive steps to protect themselves and their communities.

In conclusion, while GenAI offers tremendous benefits, the potential for misuse cannot be ignored. The challenge lies in harnessing the power of this technology while implementing safeguards to prevent its abuse. As GenAI continues to evolve, it is imperative that we remain vigilant and proactive in addressing these concerns to ensure that the technology serves the greater good without compromising ethical standards or societal well-being.

2. Exploitation of GenAI Capabilities

Impersonation

Generative AI (GenAI) has brought about remarkable advancements across various sectors, from healthcare to entertainment. However, alongside its myriad benefits, there lurks a darker side that demands scrutiny. One of the most concerning aspects of GenAI is its potential for impersonation. This capability can be exploited to create highly convincing and deceptive content, posing significant ethical, social, and security challenges.

Impersonation through GenAI involves creating digital replicas of individuals' voices, images, or even entire personas. These replicas can be so realistic that distinguishing them from genuine human interactions becomes increasingly difficult. For instance, deepfake technology, a subset of GenAI, allows for the creation of hyper-realistic videos in which people appear to say or do things they never actually did. This has severe implications for privacy, trust, and authenticity.

The technology behind these impersonations relies on sophisticated algorithms that learn from vast datasets. These datasets often include publicly available images, videos, and audio recordings. By analyzing these inputs, GenAI models can generate new content that mimics the original subjects with astonishing accuracy. While this can be beneficial for entertainment and educational purposes, it also opens the door to malicious activities.

One major concern is the potential for identity theft and fraud. Cybercriminals can use GenAI to create fake identities or mimic real individuals to deceive others. This can lead to financial scams, unauthorized access to sensitive information, and other forms of cybercrime. For example, a scammer could use a deepfake video of a company's CEO to instruct employees to transfer funds to a fraudulent account, causing significant financial losses.

Another troubling aspect is the erosion of trust in media and information. With the proliferation of deepfakes, it becomes increasingly challenging to discern factual content from manipulated media. This can lead to the spread of misinformation and disinformation, undermining public trust in news outlets, social media, and other information sources. The potential for political manipulation is particularly alarming, as deepfakes could be used to influence elections, mislead voters, or incite social unrest.

Moreover, the psychological impact on individuals who are impersonated can be profound. Victims of deepfake pornography, for instance, suffer from severe emotional distress and reputational damage. The unauthorized use of one's likeness in such a manner is a gross violation of privacy and can have long-lasting consequences for the individual's personal and professional life.

Addressing the challenges posed by GenAI impersonation requires a multi-faceted approach. Technological solutions, such as improved detection algorithms, are essential to identify and flag deepfakes. Legal frameworks also need to be updated to hold perpetrators accountable and protect victims. Public awareness campaigns can educate individuals about the risks and encourage critical evaluation of digital content.

The potential for GenAI to revolutionize industries is undeniable, but its darker capabilities cannot be ignored. Impersonation through GenAI presents a complex challenge that intersects technology, ethics, and law. As society continues to navigate the digital age, it is crucial to remain vigilant and proactive in mitigating the risks associated with this powerful technology.

Appropriated Likeness

Generative AI (GenAI) systems have rapidly evolved to create content that closely mimics human creativity. These systems can generate text, images, music, and even entire virtual environments that are indistinguishable from those crafted by human hands. However, this remarkable capability brings complex ethical and legal issues, particularly concerning the appropriation of likeness.

The core technology enabling GenAI involves training models on vast datasets, which often include copyrighted material, personal data, and other proprietary content. These datasets are crucial for the models to learn the nuances of human creativity and produce high-quality outputs. Yet, the use of such data raises significant concerns about consent and ownership. When an AI generates content that closely resembles an artist's unique style or a specific individual's likeness, questions about intellectual property rights and personal privacy become unavoidable.

One of the most contentious issues is the creation of deepfakes—highly realistic but fabricated images, videos, or audio recordings of individuals. These can be used for various purposes, ranging from entertainment to malicious activities such as identity theft, blackmail, or the dissemination of false information. The potential for harm is considerable, and current legal frameworks struggle to keep pace with the rapid advancements in GenAI technology. Users may find their digital likeness appropriated without their permission, leading to significant personal and professional repercussions.

Moreover, the commercial exploitation of generated content that mimics real individuals or established artists adds another layer of complexity. Companies and creators using GenAI can produce works that closely resemble those of renowned artists, potentially undermining the original creators' market value and infringing on their intellectual property rights. This not only affects the financial well-being of artists but also raises questions about the authenticity and integrity of creative works.

The challenge extends to the realm of data privacy. GenAI systems often require extensive data to function effectively, and this data frequently includes personal information. The extraction and use of personal data without explicit consent can lead to privacy violations, and individuals may find their personal attributes and behaviors replicated in AI-generated content. This not only breaches privacy but also risks creating a digital version of a person that can be manipulated and used in ways that the individual never intended.

Regulatory bodies and lawmakers are grappling with how to address these issues effectively. Some jurisdictions have begun to implement laws aimed at protecting individuals from unauthorized use of their likeness and personal data. However, enforcement remains challenging, especially given the global nature of the internet and the rapid development of GenAI technologies. There is a pressing need for comprehensive legal frameworks that can protect individuals and creators while fostering innovation.

Ethical considerations also play a crucial role. Developers and users of GenAI must navigate the fine line between leveraging technology for creative and beneficial purposes and respecting the rights and privacy of individuals. Ethical guidelines and industry standards are essential to ensure that GenAI is used responsibly and that the potential for misuse is minimized.

The appropriation of likeness by GenAI is a multifaceted issue that intersects with legal, ethical, and social domains. As technology continues to advance, society must carefully consider the implications and develop robust mechanisms to protect individual rights while encouraging innovation. The balance between technological progress and ethical responsibility will be key in addressing the challenges posed by the appropriation of likeness in the age of GenAI.

Sockpuppeting

Generative AI has revolutionized many aspects of our digital lives, offering unprecedented capabilities in content creation, automation, and data analysis. However, with these advancements come darker applications that exploit the technology's potential for deception and manipulation. One such nefarious use is sockpuppeting, a practice that has seen a significant increase in sophistication and scale due to GenAI.

Sockpuppeting involves creating fake online identities to deceive or manipulate public opinion, spread misinformation, or influence discussions. Traditionally, sockpuppets were manually created by individuals or small groups, but the advent of GenAI has transformed this tactic into an industrial-scale operation. AI-driven sockpuppets are not only more numerous but also more convincing, making it increasingly difficult to distinguish between genuine and fabricated personas.

Generative AI models, such as GPT-3 and its successors, possess the capability to generate human-like text that can mimic various writing styles, tones, and languages. These models can be programmed to produce content that aligns with specific agendas, making them ideal tools for creating and managing sockpuppet accounts. By leveraging these models, operators can generate a vast amount of content that appears to come from diverse, authentic sources, thereby amplifying their influence and reach.

The impact of AI-driven sockpuppeting is profound, particularly in the realms of politics, social media, and online communities. In political contexts, AI-generated sockpuppets can be used to sway public opinion, promote propaganda, and undermine trust in democratic institutions. By flooding social media platforms with coordinated messages, these sockpuppets can create the illusion of widespread support or opposition to certain policies or candidates, skewing public perception and potentially influencing election outcomes.

In online communities, AI-generated sockpuppets can infiltrate forums, comment sections, and social media groups to manipulate discussions and spread disinformation. These sockpuppets can be programmed to engage in debates, support specific viewpoints, or attack dissenting voices, effectively steering the conversation in a desired direction. This can lead to the erosion of trust within these communities, as members become increasingly uncertain about the authenticity of the interactions they encounter.

The use of GenAI for sockpuppeting also poses significant challenges for content moderation and platform governance. Traditional methods of detecting and mitigating sockpuppets, such as IP tracking and behavioral analysis, are often insufficient against AI-generated personas. These sockpuppets can be designed to exhibit varied behaviors, post from different locations, and even interact with each other in ways that mimic genuine human interactions. This makes it exceedingly difficult for automated systems and human moderators to identify and remove them.

To address the threat of AI-driven sockpuppeting, platform operators and policymakers must develop new strategies and technologies. Enhanced AI detection tools, capable of identifying subtle patterns and anomalies in content and interactions, are essential. Collaboration between platforms, governments, and cybersecurity experts can also help in sharing intelligence and developing best practices for combating this form of digital deception.

Public awareness and education are crucial components in the fight against sockpuppeting. By understanding the tactics and recognizing the signs of AI-driven manipulation, individuals can become more discerning consumers of online information. Encouraging critical thinking and media literacy can help mitigate the influence of sockpuppets and foster a more resilient digital society.

The rise of AI-driven sockpuppeting underscores the dual-edged nature of generative AI. While the technology holds immense promise for positive applications, its potential for misuse necessitates vigilant oversight and proactive measures to protect the integrity of our digital ecosystems.

Non-Consensual Intimate Imagery (NCII)

Non-consensual intimate imagery (NCII) represents a profound ethical and societal challenge in the digital age, exacerbated by advancements in generative artificial intelligence (GenAI). This phenomenon, often referred to as "revenge porn," involves the distribution of private, sexually explicit images or videos without the consent of the individual depicted. The implications are far-reaching, affecting personal privacy, mental health, and the broader social fabric.

The proliferation of sophisticated GenAI tools has made the creation and dissemination of NCII more accessible. Deep learning algorithms can fabricate realistic images and videos, known as deepfakes, which can be indistinguishable from authentic content. This technology can superimpose a person's face onto explicit material, creating a convincing yet entirely fraudulent representation. The ease with which these tools can be used accelerates the spread of NCII, complicating efforts to trace the origin and hold perpetrators accountable.

Victims of NCII often suffer severe psychological trauma. The unauthorized distribution of intimate content can lead to anxiety, depression, and even post-traumatic stress disorder. The pervasive nature of the internet means that once such images are released, they can be nearly impossible to fully remove, perpetuating the distress of the affected individuals. The societal stigma attached to these images further exacerbates the emotional toll, as victims may face social ostracization and professional repercussions.

Legal frameworks around the world are struggling to keep pace with the rapid evolution of GenAI technologies. While some jurisdictions have enacted laws specifically targeting NCII, enforcement remains a significant challenge. The anonymity provided by the internet allows perpetrators to operate with relative impunity, often crossing international borders and complicating legal recourse. Moreover, the burden of proof in such cases can be onerous, requiring victims to demonstrate the lack of consent and the identity of the perpetrator.

The role of social media platforms and internet service providers is also critical in addressing the spread of NCII. These entities are often the first line of defense in detecting and removing non-consensual content. However, their responses have been inconsistent and sometimes inadequate. Automated content moderation systems, while improving, still struggle to accurately identify and remove NCII without also censoring legitimate content. The balance between protecting user privacy and preventing the dissemination of harmful material remains a contentious issue.

Public awareness and education are essential components in combating NCII. Many individuals are unaware of the potential risks associated with sharing intimate images, even within trusted relationships. Educational initiatives can help inform the public about the dangers and encourage safer online behaviors. Additionally, support services for victims, including counseling and legal assistance, are crucial in helping them navigate the aftermath of such violations.

Technological countermeasures are also being developed to mitigate the impact of NCII. Advances in digital watermarking and blockchain technology offer potential solutions for verifying the authenticity of images and tracking their distribution. These technologies can provide a layer of protection, making it more difficult for perpetrators to manipulate and disseminate intimate content without detection.

The intersection of GenAI and NCII presents a complex challenge that requires a multifaceted approach. Legal reforms, technological innovations, corporate responsibility, and public education must all work in tandem to address this pervasive issue. The stakes are high, as the consequences of NCII extend beyond individual victims to affect societal norms and the integrity of digital spaces.

Child Sexual Abuse Material (CSAM)

Generative Artificial Intelligence (GenAI) has the potential to revolutionize numerous industries, but it also harbors the capacity for misuse. One of the gravest concerns is its involvement in the creation and dissemination of Child Sexual Abuse Material (CSAM). This issue encompasses both the ethical and legal dimensions, posing significant challenges for society.

GenAI's ability to generate realistic images, videos, and text has made it a tool for malicious actors seeking to produce CSAM. With advanced algorithms, these systems can create lifelike content that is indistinguishable from real media. This not only exacerbates the problem but also complicates the identification and removal of such material. The technology can be used to fabricate explicit content involving minors, even if no real child was harmed in the process. This raises the question of whether the creation of synthetic CSAM should be treated with the same severity as traditional forms.

The anonymity afforded by the internet allows perpetrators to share CSAM across various platforms, making detection and law enforcement efforts more difficult. Encryption and decentralized networks further complicate the tracking and apprehension of offenders. Social media platforms, file-sharing services, and the dark web are often exploited for the distribution of this illicit content. The global nature of the internet adds another layer of complexity, as laws and regulations vary significantly between jurisdictions.

Efforts to combat CSAM are multifaceted, involving technology companies, law enforcement agencies, and policymakers. Artificial Intelligence is being employed to detect and remove CSAM from online platforms. Machine learning algorithms can identify patterns and flag suspicious content, aiding in its swift removal. However, these systems are not foolproof and can sometimes result in false positives or negatives.

Continuous advancements in AI are necessary to improve accuracy and efficiency.

Legal measures are also crucial in addressing the proliferation of CSAM. Many countries have stringent laws against the creation, distribution, and possession of such material. International cooperation is essential for effective enforcement, as offenders often operate across borders. Organizations like Interpol and Europol play a vital role in coordinating efforts between nations. Additionally, there is a growing call for stronger penalties and more comprehensive legislation to tackle the evolving nature of CSAM facilitated by GenAI.

Public awareness and education are equally important. Informing parents, educators, and children about the risks and signs of CSAM can help in early detection and prevention. Advocacy groups and non-profit organizations work tirelessly to support victims and promote safer online environments. Community involvement and vigilance are key components in the fight against this heinous crime.

The ethical implications of GenAI in the context of CSAM cannot be overlooked. Developers and researchers have a responsibility to consider the potential misuse of their technologies. Ethical guidelines and frameworks are necessary to ensure that innovations in AI are aligned with societal values and do not inadvertently contribute to harm. Transparency, accountability, and ethical stewardship must be integral to the development and deployment of GenAI systems.

Addressing the issue of CSAM in the age of GenAI requires a collaborative and multi-pronged approach. Technological advancements, legal frameworks, public education, and ethical considerations must all converge to mitigate the risks and protect vulnerable populations. The challenge is formidable, but with concerted effort, progress can be made in curbing this dark facet of GenAI.

3. Falsification and Intellectual Property Infringement

Falsification Tactics

The book "The Dark Side of GenAI" delves into the multifaceted challenges and ethical quandaries posed by the rapid advancements in Generative Artificial Intelligence (GenAI). Central to these concerns is the concept of falsification tactics, which refer to the deliberate manipulation and distortion of information using GenAI technologies.

Falsification tactics encompass a range of strategies designed to deceive, mislead, or otherwise distort the truth. One of the most prominent methods involves the creation of deepfakes. These are hyper-realistic digital forgeries that can manipulate audio, video, and images in ways that make them appear authentic. The sophistication of deepfake technology has reached a point where it can convincingly alter facial expressions, voice intonations, and even the context of speech, making it extremely challenging to distinguish between genuine and fake content. This capability poses significant threats to personal privacy, political stability, and social trust.

Another critical aspect of falsification tactics is the generation of synthetic text. GenAI models, such as GPT-3, can produce text that is virtually indistinguishable from that written by humans. While this technology has beneficial applications, it can also be weaponized to create misleading articles, fake news, and deceptive social media posts. The ability to generate large volumes of coherent, persuasive text at scale makes it easier to spread misinformation and influence public opinion. This manipulation can undermine democratic processes, fuel polarization, and erode trust in legitimate information sources.

The use of GenAI in social media botnets represents another facet of falsification tactics. These botnets consist of automated accounts that can interact with users, share content, and amplify specific narratives. By leveraging GenAI, these bots can engage in more sophisticated interactions, making them harder to detect. They can create the illusion of widespread support or opposition, skewing public perception and potentially influencing real-world events. The anonymity and reach of social media platforms make them fertile ground for such deceptive activities.

Moreover, falsification tactics are not limited to overtly malicious actions. They can also be subtly integrated into marketing and advertising strategies. GenAI can be used to create personalized, persuasive content that targets individuals based on their preferences and behaviors. While this can enhance user experience, it also raises ethical concerns about manipulation and consent. The line between genuine engagement and deceptive influence becomes increasingly blurred, challenging existing regulatory frameworks and ethical standards.

The implications of falsification tactics extend beyond individual deception to societal impact. The erosion of trust in digital content can lead to a more skeptical and divided society. People may become increasingly wary of the information they encounter, potentially dismissing genuine content as fake. This skepticism can hinder effective communication, collaboration, and decision-making, with far-reaching consequences for social cohesion and governance.

Addressing the challenges posed by falsification tactics requires a multifaceted approach. Technological solutions, such as improved detection algorithms and digital watermarking, can help identify and mitigate the impact of falsified content. However, these solutions must be complemented by broader efforts to enhance digital literacy, promote ethical AI development, and establish robust regulatory frameworks. Public awareness and vigilance are crucial in recognizing and countering the deceptive potential of GenAI.

The dark side of GenAI, exemplified by falsification tactics, underscores the need for a balanced approach to technological advancement. While GenAI holds immense promise, its potential for misuse necessitates careful consideration and proactive measures to safeguard the integrity of information in the digital age.

Intellectual Property Infringement

The rise of Generative Artificial Intelligence (GenAI) has brought numerous advancements, but it has also introduced complex challenges, particularly in the realm of intellectual property (IP). One of the most pressing issues is the potential for IP infringement, as GenAI systems can inadvertently or deliberately replicate copyrighted material without proper authorization.

GenAI systems, such as those used for creating text, music, and visual art, often rely on vast datasets for training. These datasets typically include a plethora of content sourced from the internet, encompassing works protected by copyright. When a GenAI model generates new content, it may unknowingly produce material that closely resembles or even duplicates these original works. This raises significant legal and ethical concerns about the ownership and rights associated with the generated content.

The core of the problem lies in the way GenAI models learn and produce output. These systems analyze patterns in existing works to generate new content that mimics the style and structure of the input data. While this can lead to innovative and creative outputs, it also blurs the lines between inspiration and replication. For instance, a GenAI model trained on a dataset containing copyrighted music might create a new piece that sounds strikingly similar to an existing song, potentially infringing on the original artist's rights.

Another dimension of this issue is the use of copyrighted material without explicit permission during the training phase. Content creators and copyright holders may not be aware that their works are being used to train GenAI systems, leading to unauthorized exploitation of their intellectual property. This lack of transparency and consent can result in significant legal disputes and demands for compensation.

Moreover, the attribution of generated content poses additional challenges. When a GenAI system produces a work, identifying the rightful owner becomes complex. Should the credit go to the developers of the GenAI model, the creators of the original dataset, or the AI itself? This ambiguity complicates the enforcement of IP rights and the distribution of royalties, creating a murky legal landscape.

Legal frameworks worldwide are struggling to keep pace with the rapid advancements in GenAI technology. Traditional copyright laws were not designed to address the nuances of AI-generated content, leaving gaps and ambiguities. Some jurisdictions have started to propose and implement new regulations to address these challenges, but a global consensus is yet to be achieved. The evolving nature of GenAI requires continuous updates to legal standards and practices to ensure that intellectual property rights are adequately protected.

The responsibility of mitigating IP infringement does not rest solely on legal systems; developers and organizations utilizing GenAI also play a crucial role. Implementing ethical guidelines and best practices for data usage, obtaining proper licenses, and ensuring transparency in the training process are essential steps. Additionally, developing robust mechanisms to detect and prevent the replication of copyrighted material can help minimize the risk of infringement.

Addressing intellectual property infringement in the context of GenAI is a multifaceted endeavor that requires collaboration between legal experts, technologists, and policymakers. By fostering a deeper understanding of the implications and promoting responsible use of GenAI, it is possible to harness its potential while safeguarding the rights of content creators and copyright holders.

Counterfeit Content

Generative AI (GenAI) has emerged as a transformative technology capable of creating highly realistic text, images, and even videos. While its potential for innovation and creativity is immense, it also opens the door to a darker realm of counterfeit content. This issue is not merely an academic concern; it has real-world implications that affect trust, security, and the integrity of information.

The capability of GenAI to produce content that is virtually indistinguishable from that created by humans has led to an upsurge in counterfeit materials. These range from fake news articles and manipulated images to deepfakes—videos that superimpose one person's face onto another's body, creating a highly convincing but entirely false portrayal. The proliferation of such content has significant repercussions. For instance, deepfake videos have been used to discredit public figures, manipulate stock prices, and even interfere in political processes. The erosion of trust in digital media is one of the most alarming consequences, as people become increasingly skeptical about the authenticity of the information they consume.

Moreover, counterfeit content generated by GenAI can have severe implications for cybersecurity. Phishing attacks, traditionally reliant on poorly worded emails, are becoming more sophisticated. With GenAI, malicious actors can create highly convincing emails that mimic the writing style of trusted colleagues or institutions. This makes it far easier to deceive individuals into divulging sensitive information or clicking on malicious links. The potential for harm is magnified in sectors like finance and healthcare, where breaches can have catastrophic consequences.

The ability of GenAI to generate counterfeit content also poses challenges for intellectual property rights. Artists, writers, and creators of original content find themselves in a precarious position as their work can be easily replicated and distributed without consent. This not only undermines the value of original creations but also complicates the enforcement of copyright laws. Legal frameworks are struggling to keep pace with the rapid advancements in GenAI, leaving creators vulnerable to exploitation.

Counterfeit content is not limited to the digital sphere; it has tangible effects on the physical world as well. For example, counterfeit products can be marketed and sold using highly realistic advertising materials generated by GenAI. Consumers may find themselves purchasing fake goods that are virtually indistinguishable from the originals, leading to financial loss and potential harm, especially in cases involving counterfeit pharmaccuticals or safety equipment.

Addressing the issue of counterfeit content requires a multi-faceted approach. Technological solutions, such as advanced algorithms for detecting deepfakes and digital watermarks for authenticating content, are being developed. However, these are often in a constant race with the ever-evolving capabilities of GenAI. Regulatory measures and legal frameworks need to be updated to address the unique challenges posed by this technology. Public awareness and education also play a crucial role in helping individuals discern authentic content from counterfeit materials.

The rise of counterfeit content generated by GenAI is a pressing concern that demands immediate and sustained attention. As the technology continues to evolve, so too must our strategies for mitigating its darker implications. The stakes are high, affecting not just individual trust and security, but the very fabric of society's relationship with information and authenticity.

Legal Ramifications

The rapid development and deployment of Generative Artificial Intelligence (GenAI) technologies have ushered in a range of legal challenges that stakeholders must navigate. One of the primary concerns revolves around intellectual property rights. GenAI systems, capable of creating original content such as music, art, literature, and even software code, pose fundamental questions about ownership. Traditional intellectual property frameworks are ill-equipped to address scenarios where a machine, rather than a human, is the creator. This ambiguity raises the critical issue of who holds the copyright: the user of the GenAI, the developer of the GenAI system, or the entity that owns the data used to train the AI.

Privacy concerns also loom large. GenAI systems often require vast amounts of data to function effectively. This data is frequently harvested from various sources, including social media, public records, and other digital footprints. The collection, storage, and utilization of such data must comply with existing privacy laws, such as the General Data Protection Regulation (GDPR) in Europe and the California Consumer Privacy Act (CCPA) in the United States. Non-compliance can lead to severe penalties and damage to organizational reputations. Furthermore, the potential for GenAI to generate deepfakes and other realistic but false content exacerbates the risk of privacy violations, as individuals may find their likenesses and personal information exploited without consent.

Liability is another significant legal issue. When GenAI systems malfunction or produce harmful outputs, determining who is responsible can be complex. Traditional legal principles of liability may not clearly apply, especially when the harm is indirect or the result of autonomous decision-making by the AI. This complexity is particularly evident in sectors like healthcare, where GenAI is used for diagnostics and treatment planning. Errors in these high-stakes environments can have life-or-death consequences, and assigning liability becomes a convoluted task involving multiple parties, including software developers, data providers, and end-users.

Employment law is also being tested by the advent of GenAI. As these systems become more capable, they are increasingly used to perform tasks previously done by humans. This automation can lead to job displacement and raises questions about the rights of workers. Legal frameworks must evolve to address issues such as fair compensation, retraining programs, and the ethical implications of widespread automation. Additionally, the use of GenAI in hiring processes, such as resume screening and interview analysis, introduces concerns about bias and discrimination. Employers must ensure that their use of GenAI complies with equal employment opportunity laws and does not perpetuate existing biases.

Finally, regulatory oversight is crucial to ensure that GenAI technologies are developed and deployed responsibly. Governments and regulatory bodies worldwide are grappling with how to create effective regulations that balance innovation with public safety and ethical considerations. Existing laws often lag behind technological advancements, necessitating proactive measures to update and create new regulations. International cooperation is also essential, as GenAI operates across borders, making unilateral regulatory efforts less effective.

The legal landscape surrounding GenAI is intricate and evolving. It requires continuous dialogue among technologists, legal experts, policymakers, and the public to navigate these challenges effectively. The stakes are high, and the outcomes will shape the future of technology and society.

Case Studies

The implications of General Artificial Intelligence (GenAI) are best understood through real-world examples that highlight both its potential and its dangers. Examining specific case studies provides a grounded perspective on how GenAI can influence various sectors, from healthcare to security, and underscores the ethical dilemmas it presents.

One notable case involves a healthcare system that integrated GenAI to improve diagnostic accuracy and patient care. The AI was trained on extensive datasets, including medical records, imaging, and genetic information. Initially, the results were promising; the system accurately identified early-stage diseases, suggesting personalized treatment plans that led to improved patient outcomes. However, issues emerged when biases in the training data resulted in misdiagnoses for minority groups. These errors were not immediately apparent, causing significant delays in appropriate treatment for affected individuals. The case underscores the necessity for diverse and representative datasets to ensure fair and accurate AI applications in healthcare.

In another instance, a financial institution employed GenAI to enhance its fraud detection mechanisms. The AI analyzed transaction patterns and flagged suspicious activities with unprecedented speed and accuracy. This led to a significant reduction in fraudulent transactions and financial losses. Yet, the system also generated false positives, affecting legitimate customers whose accounts were wrongly flagged and temporarily frozen. The inconvenience and reputational damage caused by these errors highlighted the need for human oversight, even in highly automated systems.

The deployment of GenAI in law enforcement offers another illustrative example. A city police department adopted AI for predictive policing, aiming to allocate resources more efficiently and reduce crime rates. The AI analyzed crime data to predict where future incidents were likely to occur. Initially, crime rates dropped in targeted areas, suggesting the system's efficacy. Over time, however, it became clear that the AI disproportionately targeted minority neighborhoods, exacerbating existing tensions and perpetuating systemic biases. This case points to the critical importance of transparency and accountability in AI systems used for public safety.

The use of GenAI in social media platforms for content moderation is also noteworthy. Platforms utilized AI to identify and remove harmful content, such as hate speech and misinformation, more effectively than human moderators. While this improved the overall user experience and safety, it also raised concerns about free speech and censorship. The AI sometimes misclassified content, leading to the removal of legitimate posts and the suppression of certain viewpoints. This scenario highlights the delicate balance between maintaining a safe online environment and protecting individual rights.

Lastly, the military's exploration of GenAI for autonomous weapons systems presents profound ethical challenges. These systems are designed to make split-second decisions in combat scenarios, potentially reducing human casualties. However, the possibility of AI making life-and-death decisions without human intervention raises significant moral and legal questions. The risk of malfunction or misuse, leading to unintended consequences, further complicates the debate over the deployment of such technologies.

These case studies illustrate the dual-edged nature of GenAI. While it holds the promise of revolutionizing various fields, its implementation is fraught with challenges that must be carefully navigated. Ethical considerations, data integrity, and the need for human oversight are critical factors that must be addressed to harness the benefits of GenAI while mitigating its risks.

4. Scaling, Amplification, Targeting, and Personalization

Scaling Misuse Tactics

Generative AI (GenAI) has transformed numerous industries with its potential to automate tasks, generate creative content, and enhance decision-making processes. However, this powerful technology is not without its risks. One of the most concerning aspects is the potential for misuse, particularly when such misuse is scaled. Understanding the ways in which bad actors can exploit GenAI at scale is crucial for developing effective countermeasures.

The democratization of AI tools has made it easier for individuals and organizations to access powerful generative models. While this has accelerated innovation, it also means that malicious entities can harness these tools for nefarious purposes. One prominent misuse tactic involves the creation of deepfakes. These hyper-realistic digital forgeries can be used to spread misinformation, manipulate public opinion, or extort individuals. When scaled, the impact of deepfakes can be devastating, undermining trust in media and eroding societal cohesion.

Another area of concern is the automated generation of disinformation. GenAI can be employed to produce vast quantities of fake news articles, social media posts, and other forms of content designed to mislead the public. By leveraging AI's ability to mimic human writing styles and generate believable narratives, malicious actors can flood information channels with falsehoods, making it difficult for individuals to discern truth from fiction. This tactic becomes particularly potent when coordinated across multiple platforms, amplifying the reach and impact of disinformation campaigns.

Cybercriminals are also leveraging GenAI to enhance their phishing attacks. Traditional phishing methods often rely on generic, poorly written emails that are easier to identify and block. However, with GenAI, attackers can generate highly personalized and convincing messages that are tailored to individual targets. These AI-generated phishing attempts can include specific details about the target's life, making them far more effective. When scaled, this tactic can lead to widespread data breaches and financial losses.

The scalability of GenAI misuse extends to the realm of cyber warfare. Nation-states and organized cybercriminal groups can deploy AI-driven attacks on critical infrastructure, such as power grids, financial systems, and communication networks. By automating the reconnaissance and exploitation phases of cyberattacks, GenAI enables these entities to launch large-scale operations with unprecedented speed and precision. The potential for widespread disruption and damage is significant, posing a severe threat to national security.

The rapid advancement of GenAI also raises ethical concerns in the realm of surveillance and privacy. Governments and corporations can use AI to analyze vast amounts of data, identifying patterns and behaviors that would be impossible to detect manually. While this can be beneficial for crime prevention and market analysis, it also opens the door to intrusive surveillance practices. When scaled, these capabilities can lead to a surveillance state where privacy is eroded, and individuals' freedoms are compromised.

Addressing the challenges posed by scaled misuse of GenAI requires a multifaceted approach. Regulatory frameworks must be developed to govern the ethical use of AI, while technology companies need to implement robust safeguards and detection mechanisms. Public awareness and education are also essential, empowering individuals to recognize and respond to AI-driven threats. By understanding the tactics used to misuse GenAI at scale, society can take proactive steps to mitigate the risks and harness the technology's full potential for good.

Amplification Strategies

Generative Artificial Intelligence (GenAI) is a transformative technology with the potential to reshape various facets of society. However, it also harbors the capacity to amplify negative aspects, which warrants a thorough examination. One critical area of concern is how GenAI can be utilized to amplify misinformation and disinformation. This phenomenon has far-reaching implications for public trust, social stability, and even democratic processes.

The deployment of GenAI in the realm of information dissemination introduces a new level of sophistication to the creation and spread of false information. Traditional methods of generating misinformation often require significant human effort and are relatively easy to identify and debunk. GenAI, however, can produce highly convincing text, images, and videos at scale, making it increasingly difficult for average users to distinguish between what is real and what is fabricated. This capability is especially concerning when considering the speed at which information spreads on social media platforms.

The algorithms that power GenAI are trained on vast datasets, which include both accurate and inaccurate information. This inherent characteristic means that the outputs generated by these models can sometimes be misleading or entirely false. When such outputs are disseminated, they can contribute to the spread of misinformation, either unintentionally or as part of coordinated disinformation campaigns. The latter is particularly troubling as it involves the deliberate use of false information to deceive and manipulate public opinion or obscure the truth.

Moreover, GenAI can be exploited to create deepfakes—highly realistic but entirely fabricated videos and audio recordings. These deepfakes can be used to impersonate public figures, spread false narratives, and incite unrest. For instance, a deepfake video of a political leader making inflammatory statements could potentially lead to significant social and political consequences. The ability to produce such convincing forgeries at scale further complicates efforts to maintain the integrity of information in the digital age.

Another amplification strategy involves the use of GenAI to create and manage large numbers of fake social media accounts. These accounts can be used to generate and spread false information, create the illusion of consensus, and manipulate public opinion. By automating the process of content creation and dissemination, GenAI makes it possible to flood social media platforms with misleading information, thereby drowning out legitimate voices and eroding public trust.

The challenge of countering these amplification strategies is significant. Traditional fact-checking methods are often too slow to keep up with the rapid spread of misinformation enabled by GenAI. Additionally, the sheer volume of content generated by these models can overwhelm existing moderation systems. This necessitates the development of more sophisticated detection and mitigation techniques, including the use of AI to identify and flag potentially false content in real-time.

Despite these challenges, there are promising avenues for addressing the negative impacts of GenAI on information integrity. Collaborative efforts between technology companies, governments, and civil society organizations are crucial. These stakeholders can work together to develop and implement policies and technologies that mitigate the risks associated with GenAI. Education and awareness campaigns can also play a vital role in helping the public recognize and critically evaluate the information they encounter online.

In essence, while GenAI offers significant benefits, it also poses serious risks when used to amplify misinformation and disinformation. Understanding and addressing these risks is essential to harnessing the positive potential of this technology while safeguarding the integrity of information in our digital society.

Targeting Techniques

Artificial Intelligence, particularly Generative AI (GenAI), has made significant strides in various sectors, enhancing efficiency and innovation. However, its capabilities also present new challenges and ethical dilemmas, particularly in the realm of targeting techniques. These methods, which leverage the power of AI to identify, segment, and reach specific groups or individuals, have profound implications for privacy, security, and societal dynamics.

One of the primary techniques employed in targeting is data mining. GenAI systems can analyze vast amounts of data from multiple sources, including social media, browsing history, and purchase records, to construct detailed profiles of individuals. This profiling allows for highly personalized marketing strategies, as companies can tailor their advertisements to the specific preferences and behaviors of users. While this can enhance user experience and engagement, it raises significant concerns about the extent of surveillance and the potential for manipulative practices.

Another technique involves predictive analytics, where GenAI systems use historical data to predict future behaviors and trends. This approach is particularly potent in sectors like finance and healthcare, where anticipating market movements or patient needs can lead to substantial benefits.

However, the same predictive power can be exploited for more nefarious purposes, such as political manipulation or discriminatory practices. For instance, by predicting voting behaviors, political campaigns can target specific demographics with tailored messages, potentially skewing public opinion or exacerbating societal divisions.

Social network analysis is also a crucial tool in the arsenal of GenAI targeting techniques. By mapping and analyzing the relationships and interactions within a network, AI can identify key influencers and opinion leaders. This technique is invaluable for marketing and public relations, as influencing a few central figures can lead to widespread dissemination of a message. Yet, this capability can be misused to spread misinformation or propaganda, as seen in various disinformation campaigns.

Behavioral targeting, which focuses on tracking users' online activities to deliver relevant ads, is another widespread application. GenAI enhances this by not only tracking but also interpreting the context and sentiment behind interactions. This allows for even more precise targeting, but it also means that users are constantly monitored and their data constantly analyzed. The invasive nature of this technique poses significant ethical questions regarding consent and the right to privacy.

Location-based targeting leverages data from mobile devices to deliver content based on a user's geographical location. This can be incredibly useful for local businesses and emergency services. However, the constant tracking of individuals' movements raises severe privacy concerns and potential misuse by malicious actors, such as stalkers or authoritarian regimes.

The ethical implications of these targeting techniques are profound. While they offer undeniable benefits in terms of efficiency and personalization, they also pose significant risks. The potential for abuse is high, whether through invasive surveillance, manipulation, or discrimination. As GenAI continues to evolve, it is crucial to develop robust ethical guidelines and regulatory frameworks to mitigate these risks.

In understanding the dark side of GenAI, it becomes clear that the same technologies that drive innovation and progress can also be wielded for less benign purposes. The challenge lies in balancing the benefits of advanced targeting techniques with the need for ethical considerations and protections against misuse.

Personalization in Attacks

The increasing sophistication of generative AI (GenAI) technologies has opened new avenues for cybercriminals to exploit. One of the most alarming trends is the personalization of attacks, where malicious actors harness AI to tailor their schemes to individual targets. This chapter delves into how personalization in cyberattacks has evolved and the implications it carries for both individuals and organizations.

Personalized attacks leverage vast amounts of data to create highly targeted and convincing scams. These attacks often begin with the collection of personal information from various sources, including social media profiles, public records, and previously breached databases. By analyzing this data, attackers can craft messages that appear legitimate and relevant to the recipient, significantly increasing the likelihood of success.

Phishing is one of the most common forms of personalized attacks. Traditional phishing attempts often rely on generic messages sent to a large number of recipients, hoping that some will take the bait. However, with the advent of GenAI, these attacks have become increasingly sophisticated. AI algorithms can now generate emails that mimic the writing style of a specific individual or organization, making it difficult for even the most vigilant users to detect the deception. These personalized phishing emails may reference specific details about the target's life or work, such as recent transactions, upcoming meetings, or even personal interests, making them highly convincing.

Another area where personalization is being exploited is in social engineering attacks. Cybercriminals use AI to gather information about their targets and create detailed profiles. These profiles can include information about the target's job, hobbies, family, and social connections. Armed with this knowledge, attackers can craft persuasive narratives that exploit the target's trust and familiarity. For example, an attacker might pose as a colleague or friend, using information gleaned from social media to establish credibility and manipulate the target into divulging sensitive information or performing actions that compromise security.

Ransomware attacks have also seen a shift towards personalization. In the past, ransomware was often distributed indiscriminately, with attackers hoping to infect as many devices as possible. Today, cybercriminals are using AI to identify high-value targets and tailor their attacks accordingly. By focusing on individuals or organizations with the means to pay substantial ransoms, attackers can maximize their profits. Personalized ransomware attacks may also involve threats that are specifically designed to pressure the victim into paying, such as the release of sensitive personal information or the disruption of critical business operations.

The implications of personalized attacks are profound. For individuals, the increased sophistication of these attacks means that traditional security measures, such as antivirus software and firewalls, may no longer be sufficient. Users must be more vigilant and skeptical of unsolicited communications, even if they appear to come from trusted sources. For organizations, the rise of personalized attacks underscores the need for comprehensive cybersecurity strategies that include employee training, robust data protection measures, and advanced threat detection systems.

As GenAI continues to evolve, the landscape of cyber threats will undoubtedly become more complex. Understanding the methods and motivations behind personalized attacks is crucial for developing effective defenses. By staying informed and proactive, individuals and organizations can better navigate the challenges posed by the dark side of GenAI.

Impact on Society

Generative AI, or GenAI, has introduced myriad advancements across various fields, but its implications for society are profound and multifaceted. While the technology promises significant benefits, it also poses complex challenges that need careful consideration.

One of the most immediate impacts of GenAI is on the job market. Automation and AI-driven processes are already transforming industries, from manufacturing to customer service. GenAI can perform tasks that were once thought to require human creativity and intuition, such as writing articles, creating art, and composing music. This shift raises concerns about job displacement and the future of work. Many fear that as GenAI becomes more sophisticated, it will render certain professions obsolete, leading to widespread unemployment and economic instability.

Moreover, the ethical ramifications of GenAI cannot be ignored. The ability of these systems to generate content that is indistinguishable from human-created work raises questions about authenticity and intellectual property. Artists, writers, and musicians may find their livelihoods threatened by AI-generated works that mimic their styles and techniques. Additionally, the potential for misuse is significant. Deepfakes, for instance, are a troubling application of GenAI, capable of creating realistic but false images and videos. These can be used to spread misinformation, manipulate public opinion, and even commit fraud.

Privacy is another major concern. GenAI systems often require vast amounts of data to function effectively. This data is typically harvested from users, sometimes without their explicit consent. The collection and use of such data raise significant privacy issues, as individuals may unknowingly contribute to datasets that train these AI systems. The potential for abuse is considerable, especially if this data falls into the wrong hands or is used for purposes beyond those originally intended.

The societal impact of GenAI also extends to issues of bias and fairness. AI systems are only as good as the data they are trained on. If the training data contains biases, the AI will inevitably reproduce and potentially amplify those biases. This can lead to discriminatory practices in areas like hiring, law enforcement, and lending. Efforts to mitigate these biases are ongoing, but the challenge is substantial and requires continuous vigilance.

On a broader scale, GenAI has the potential to alter human interactions and relationships. The line between human and machine-generated content is becoming increasingly blurred. This can lead to a sense of alienation and mistrust among individuals who may find it difficult to distinguish between genuine human interactions and AI-generated ones. The authenticity of online communication, social media interactions, and even news sources is at risk, potentially eroding trust in digital platforms.

Despite these challenges, it is important to recognize the positive contributions of GenAI. It has the potential to revolutionize healthcare by assisting in diagnostics and treatment planning, enhance educational tools, and provide personalized learning experiences. In the creative industries, it can serve as a powerful tool for artists and writers, offering new ways to explore and experiment with their craft.

The societal impact of GenAI is a double-edged sword, presenting both opportunities and risks. As the technology continues to evolve, it is crucial for policymakers, technologists, and society at large to engage in ongoing dialogue about its implications. Responsible development and deployment of GenAI will be key to harnessing its benefits while mitigating its potential harms.

5. Compromise of GenAI Systems

Adversarial Inputs

Generative AI systems, often hailed for their innovative capabilities, have a less explored but crucial aspect: their vulnerability to adversarial inputs. These inputs, intentionally crafted to deceive AI models, can lead to unpredictable and often harmful outcomes. Understanding the nature and impact of these adversarial inputs is essential for developing robust AI systems that can withstand malicious attacks.

Adversarial inputs are carefully designed perturbations added to the data fed into AI systems. These perturbations are usually imperceptible to human observers but can significantly alter the AI's behavior. For instance, a slight modification in the pixel values of an image can cause a well-trained image recognition model to misclassify a stop sign as a yield sign. Such manipulations pose serious risks, particularly in critical applications like autonomous driving, where misclassification can lead to accidents.

The creation of adversarial inputs involves exploiting the inherent weaknesses in the AI model's learning process. Generative AI models, which are trained on vast amounts of data to generate new content, often rely on patterns and correlations within the data. Adversaries can identify and manipulate these patterns to produce inputs that the model interprets incorrectly. This manipulation can be as subtle as changing a few pixels in an image or as complex as altering the structure of a sentence in a text-based model.

The implications of adversarial inputs extend beyond mere misclassification. In the context of natural language processing (NLP), adversarial attacks can manipulate AI-generated text to spread misinformation or biased narratives. This can have far-reaching consequences, especially in areas like journalism, where the integrity of information is paramount. By subtly altering the wording or context of a generated article, adversaries can influence public opinion and potentially disrupt social harmony.

Moreover, adversarial inputs can compromise the security and privacy of AI systems. In scenarios where AI models are used for authentication, such as facial recognition or voice verification, adversarial attacks can bypass security measures, granting unauthorized access to sensitive information. This not only undermines the trust in AI systems but also poses significant risks to personal and organizational security.

Mitigating the risks associated with adversarial inputs requires a multi-faceted approach. One strategy is to improve the robustness of AI models through adversarial training. This involves exposing the model to adversarial examples during the training phase, enabling it to learn how to recognize and resist such inputs. Another approach is to develop detection mechanisms that can identify and filter out adversarial inputs before they reach the AI system. These mechanisms often rely on anomaly detection techniques, which flag inputs that deviate from the norm.

Collaboration between AI researchers, practitioners, and policymakers is crucial in addressing the challenges posed by adversarial inputs. Establishing standards and guidelines for AI development and deployment can help ensure that systems are designed with security and robustness in mind. Additionally, ongoing research into new attack vectors and defense strategies is essential for staying ahead of adversaries who continuously evolve their tactics.

In the realm of generative AI, where creativity and innovation are celebrated, it is imperative to remain vigilant about the potential dark sides. Adversarial inputs represent a significant threat that can undermine the benefits of AI technologies. By understanding and addressing these challenges, we can work towards building AI systems that are not only intelligent but also resilient and trustworthy.

Prompt Injections

GenAI, while a marvel of modern technology, harbors vulnerabilities that can be exploited in ways that are both unexpected and nefarious. One such vulnerability is the phenomenon known as prompt injections. These are deliberate manipulations of the input provided to a generative AI system, designed to coerce it into producing unintended or harmful outputs. By understanding the mechanics and potential impacts of prompt injections, we can better appreciate the risks posed by these sophisticated attacks.

At the heart of generative AI systems lies the concept of prompts—inputs that guide the AI in generating responses. These prompts are typically designed to be straightforward and benign, such as asking the AI to generate a poem or answer a question. However, the AI's reliance on these prompts also makes it susceptible to manipulation. Malicious actors can craft inputs that appear innocuous but contain hidden instructions or code that exploit the AI's processing algorithms.

For example, an attacker might input a seemingly innocent query that includes covert directives. The AI, following its programmed instructions, processes the entire prompt, including the hidden commands, and generates output based on the manipulative input. This can lead to the AI producing content that is misleading, inappropriate, or even dangerous. The subtlety of prompt injections makes them particularly insidious, as they can be difficult to detect and prevent.

The implications of prompt injections are far-reaching. In the realm of misinformation, attackers could use prompt injections to generate convincing fake news, deepening the spread of false information. In more malicious scenarios, prompt injections could be used to produce harmful content, such as hate speech or incitement to violence, which the AI would otherwise be programmed to avoid. This undermines the trust and reliability of generative AI systems, posing significant risks to both users and society at large.

Moreover, prompt injections can compromise the integrity of AI-driven decision-making processes. In fields such as finance, healthcare, and law, where AI systems are increasingly relied upon for critical decisions, prompt injections could lead to erroneous conclusions or actions. This not only jeopardizes the outcomes of these decisions but also erodes confidence in the use of AI for important tasks.

Addressing the threat of prompt injections requires a multifaceted approach. Developers must enhance the robustness of AI systems, ensuring that they can recognize and mitigate manipulative inputs. This involves improving the AI's ability to discern context and detect anomalies in prompts. Additionally, continuous monitoring and updating of AI models are essential to stay ahead of evolving tactics used by malicious actors.

User education also plays a crucial role in combating prompt injections. Users should be aware of the potential risks and be encouraged to scrutinize the inputs they provide to AI systems. By fostering a culture of vigilance and responsibility, the likelihood of successful prompt injections can be reduced.

In the broader context of AI ethics and governance, the issue of prompt injections underscores the need for comprehensive regulations and guidelines. Policymakers and industry leaders must collaborate to establish standards that ensure the safe and ethical use of generative AI. This includes developing frameworks for accountability and transparency, as well as mechanisms for reporting and addressing AI-related vulnerabilities.

By shining a light on the dark side of generative AI, specifically through the lens of prompt injections, we can better prepare for and mitigate the risks associated with this powerful technology.

Jailbreaking

Amid the rapidly evolving landscape of generative artificial intelligence (GenAI), the concept of jailbreaking has emerged as a contentious and intriguing phenomenon. In essence, jailbreaking refers to the process of circumventing the built-in restrictions and safety protocols of AI systems to unlock their full, unrestrained capabilities. While this might sound like a technical feat reserved for a niche group of enthusiasts, its implications are far-reaching and multifaceted, impacting everything from ethical considerations to security concerns.

Jailbreaking AI systems often involves manipulating the algorithms and code that govern their behavior. These manipulations can range from relatively benign tweaks to more profound alterations that fundamentally change how the AI operates. For instance, a user might alter the parameters of a language model to bypass content filters, allowing the AI to generate text that it was originally programmed to avoid. Such modifications can be achieved through various means, including exploiting vulnerabilities in the software or employing sophisticated reverse-engineering techniques.

The motivations behind jailbreaking AI systems are diverse. On one hand, researchers and developers might engage in this practice to explore the limits of AI technology, pushing it beyond its intended use cases to gain deeper insights. This experimental approach can lead to breakthroughs in understanding AI's potential and limitations. On the other hand, there are those who seek to jailbreak AI for less altruistic reasons. Malicious actors might exploit these techniques to create harmful content, spread misinformation, or even deploy AI-driven cyberattacks. The dual-use nature of AI jailbreaking makes it a double-edged sword, capable of both advancing knowledge and causing significant harm.

Ethical considerations play a crucial role in the discourse surrounding AI jailbreaking. The act of deliberately bypassing safety protocols raises questions about responsibility and accountability. Who is to blame if a jailbroken AI system generates harmful or offensive content? Is it the original developers who created the AI, the individuals who modified it, or the users who deployed it inappropriately? These questions are not easily answered and highlight the complex interplay between technology and human agency.

Moreover, the security implications of AI jailbreaking cannot be underestimated. By disabling or circumventing safety features, jailbroken AI systems can become vectors for a variety of cyber threats. For instance, an AI that has been modified to ignore ethical guidelines could be used to generate convincing phishing emails, deepfake videos, or other forms of digital deception. The potential for such misuse necessitates robust countermeasures and a vigilant approach to AI security.

Regulatory frameworks are beginning to address the challenges posed by AI jailbreaking. Governments and institutions are exploring policies and guidelines to mitigate the risks associated with this practice. These efforts aim to strike a balance between fostering innovation and ensuring that AI technologies are used responsibly. However, the rapid pace of AI development often outstrips the ability of regulatory bodies to keep up, leading to a dynamic and sometimes contentious regulatory landscape.

In light of these complexities, it is clear that jailbreaking represents a significant aspect of the dark side of GenAI. While it offers opportunities for innovation and deeper understanding, it also poses substantial risks that must be carefully managed. The ongoing dialogue between developers, ethicists, and policymakers will play a crucial role in navigating the challenges and opportunities presented by this phenomenon.

Model Diversion

The landscape of artificial intelligence has been dramatically transformed by the advent of generative AI (GenAI), which can create text, images, audio, and even video from minimal input. While the technology offers groundbreaking possibilities, it also brings with it a set of ethical and practical concerns that demand scrutiny. One of the most pressing issues is the diversion of AI models for purposes other than those initially intended, a phenomenon that can have far-reaching consequences.

When developers create AI models, they often have specific applications in mind, such as language translation, automated customer service, or medical diagnostics. However, once these models are released into the world, they can be repurposed for entirely different uses, sometimes with malicious intent. This model diversion can occur for several reasons, including the open-source nature of many AI frameworks, the widespread availability of computational power, and the increasing sophistication of users who can re-engineer these models.

One of the most troubling aspects of model diversion is its potential for misuse in generating disinformation. For instance, a model designed to assist in writing articles can be diverted to create fake news or propaganda. These AI-generated pieces can be highly convincing, making it difficult for readers to discern fact from fiction. The rapid dissemination of such content can have serious implications for public opinion, elections, and even national security.

Another area of concern is the use of diverted models in cybercrime. AI can be employed to automate phishing attacks, craft highly personalized scam messages, or even break into secure systems by guessing passwords. The same algorithms that are designed to help businesses understand customer behavior can be diverted to predict human vulnerabilities, making cyber-attacks more effective and harder to defend against.

The healthcare sector is not immune to the risks of model diversion. AI models initially developed for diagnosing diseases or recommending treatments can be repurposed for less altruistic aims. For example, a model could be diverted to create fake medical records, manipulate insurance claims, or even design harmful biological agents. The implications for public health and safety are staggering, necessitating stringent oversight and regulation.

Beyond these immediate dangers, model diversion also raises questions about intellectual property and accountability. When a model is diverted, who is responsible for the consequences? The original developers, the entity that diverted the model, or the platform that hosted it? These questions are not easily answered, and they complicate the ethical landscape of AI development and deployment.

The open-source movement, while democratizing access to advanced technologies, also unwittingly facilitates model diversion. Open-source AI frameworks provide the building blocks for anyone with the requisite skills to create powerful models. While this fosters innovation, it also lowers the barrier for potential misuse. Balancing the benefits of open access with the need for security and ethical considerations is a delicate task that requires collaborative effort from the AI community, policymakers, and society at large.

Technical solutions to mitigate model diversion are being explored. These include watermarking AI outputs to trace their origin, implementing robust access controls, and developing algorithms that can detect and prevent misuse. However, technology alone cannot solve the problem. A comprehensive approach that includes ethical guidelines, regulatory frameworks, and public awareness is essential.

Model diversion is a multifaceted issue that underscores the darker potentials of generative AI. While the technology holds immense promise, its responsible use is imperative to prevent unintended and potentially harmful consequences. As we continue to advance in the field of AI, vigilance and proactive measures are crucial to ensuring that the benefits of GenAI are realized without compromising ethical standards and public safety.

Model Extraction

Model extraction is a pressing concern in the realm of Generative AI (GenAI), raising significant ethical and security issues. This phenomenon involves the unauthorized replication of a proprietary AI model, often achieved by leveraging access to the model's outputs. Model extraction not only compromises intellectual property but also poses risks to data privacy and system integrity.

The mechanics of model extraction are multifaceted. Attackers typically start by querying the target model, treating it as a black box. By systematically feeding it inputs and observing the outputs, they gather valuable insights into the model's behavior. These insights are then used to reconstruct a surrogate model that mimics the original. This surrogate can be nearly as effective as the proprietary model, allowing the attacker to exploit it for various purposes without needing access to the original training data or the model's internal architecture.

A critical aspect of model extraction is the notion of query efficiency. Attackers aim to extract a model using the fewest possible queries to minimize detection and reduce costs. Advanced techniques such as active learning and reinforcement learning can optimize this process. Active learning enables the attacker to select the most informative queries, while reinforcement learning helps in refining the extraction strategy based on past interactions with the model.

The implications of model extraction are profound. For businesses, it translates to a direct loss of competitive advantage. Companies invest substantial resources in developing sophisticated AI models, and unauthorized replication undermines this investment. Furthermore, the extracted model can be used to create products or services that compete unfairly with the original, eroding market share and profitability.

From a security perspective, model extraction opens the door to more severe attacks. Once an attacker has a surrogate model, they can exploit it to uncover vulnerabilities in the original system. For instance, adversarial attacks, where slight perturbations in input data lead to incorrect outputs, become easier to orchestrate. The surrogate model serves as a testing ground for perfecting these perturbations before deploying them against the original model.

Ethical considerations also come to the fore. The extracted model may be used in ways that the original creators did not intend or approve. This misuse can range from generating misleading information to creating deepfakes, thereby amplifying the potential for social harm. Moreover, the lack of accountability in the use of extracted models complicates the enforcement of ethical guidelines and regulations.

Mitigating the risks associated with model extraction requires a multi-pronged approach. One effective strategy is the implementation of robust access controls. Limiting the number and type of queries that can be made to the model can significantly hinder extraction efforts. Additionally, monitoring and analyzing query patterns can help in early detection of extraction attempts. Techniques like rate limiting and anomaly detection can flag suspicious activities, enabling timely intervention.

Another promising avenue is the use of defensive distillation, a process that modifies the original model to be less susceptible to extraction. By training the model in a way that smooths out its decision boundaries, defensive distillation makes it harder for attackers to infer precise model behavior from outputs. This approach, however, comes with trade-offs in terms of model performance and complexity.

Legal and regulatory frameworks also play a crucial role. Strengthening intellectual property laws to encompass AI models can provide a deterrent against unauthorized replication. Furthermore, establishing industry standards for model security and ethical use can foster a more secure and responsible AI ecosystem.

Model extraction remains a formidable challenge in the landscape of GenAI. Addressing it requires concerted efforts from technologists, businesses, and policymakers alike. As AI continues to evolve, so too must the strategies to safeguard its integrity and ethical use.

6. Steganography and Poisoning

Steganography Techniques

Steganography, an age-old method of concealing information within seemingly innocuous data, has found a new realm of application in the era of Generative AI (GenAI). This technique, which dates back to ancient civilizations where messages were hidden within wax tablets or under the guise of harmless letters, has evolved dramatically with the advent of digital technology. In the context of GenAI, steganography serves as a potent tool for both benign and malicious purposes, capitalizing on the sophisticated capabilities of AI-generated content.

In the digital age, steganography involves embedding hidden information within digital media such as images, audio files, and even text. This concealed data remains undetectable under normal scrutiny, revealing itself only through specific algorithms or keys. GenAI, with its prowess in creating highly realistic and complex media, enhances this concealment process, making the hidden data even more elusive.

One of the primary techniques in digital steganography is Least Significant Bit (LSB) insertion. This method modifies the least significant bits of pixel values in an image or audio samples in a sound file to embed hidden information. The changes are subtle enough to be imperceptible to the human senses, yet they can encode significant amounts of data. GenAI can generate images or audio files with such modifications inherently built-in, making detection exceedingly difficult without specialized tools.

Another advanced technique involves the use of algorithms like Discrete Cosine Transform (DCT) or Discrete Wavelet Transform (DWT). These methods transform the media into a different domain, where the hidden data can be embedded within the coefficients of the transformed representation. When the media is converted back to its original form, the hidden data remains intact yet concealed. GenAI's ability to manipulate data at a granular level allows for even more sophisticated implementations of these techniques, embedding data in ways that are resistant to conventional detection methods.

Text steganography has also seen significant advancements with GenAI. Traditional methods often relied on altering the formatting of text or using specific patterns of words or letters. However, with AI-generated text, the possibilities expand considerably. Techniques such as using synonym substitution, where certain words are replaced with their synonyms to encode information, or generating entire paragraphs that contain hidden data within the structure and choice of words, become feasible. The natural language generation capabilities of GenAI ensure that these modifications remain coherent and natural, making detection by human readers almost impossible.

Moreover, GenAI facilitates the creation of deepfakes—highly realistic but artificial media. These deepfakes can serve as carriers for steganographic content. For instance, a deepfake video might contain hidden messages within the pixel data or the audio stream, masked by the complexity and realism of the generated content. The sophistication of GenAI-generated deepfakes adds an additional layer of obfuscation, making the hidden data even more challenging to uncover.

While steganography in the context of GenAI presents significant opportunities for secure communication and data protection, it also poses substantial risks. The same techniques that can safeguard sensitive information can be exploited for nefarious purposes, such as covert communication by malicious actors or the distribution of hidden malware. The dual-use nature of steganography in GenAI underscores the importance of developing robust detection and countermeasure techniques to mitigate potential threats.

Understanding the intricacies of steganography techniques in the realm of GenAI is crucial for both leveraging its benefits and addressing its challenges. As AI continues to evolve, so too will the methods of concealing and detecting hidden information, shaping the landscape of digital security and privacy.

Poisoning Attacks

Poisoning attacks represent a particularly insidious threat in the realm of generative artificial intelligence (GenAI). These attacks aim to compromise the integrity of a machine learning model by subtly corrupting the training data it relies on. Unlike other forms of cyberattacks that may exploit vulnerabilities in code or hardware, poisoning attacks target the very foundation of the model's intelligence: its data.

The mechanics of a poisoning attack are both sophisticated and devious. An adversary introduces maliciously crafted data into the training set with the objective of manipulating the model's behavior. This corrupted data can be designed to degrade the model's overall performance or to trigger specific, erroneous outputs under certain conditions. For instance, in a facial recognition system, an attacker might insert subtly altered images that cause the system to misidentify individuals, thereby undermining its reliability and security.

One of the most challenging aspects of defending against poisoning attacks is the subtlety with which they can be executed. The injected malicious data often appears benign and blends seamlessly with legitimate data, making it difficult to detect. This stealthiness is a significant advantage for adversaries, as even a small percentage of poisoned data can have a disproportionate impact on the model's performance.

The consequences of successful poisoning attacks can be dire. In the context of GenAI, where models might generate text, images, or other media, the implications are vast. A poisoned model could produce biased or harmful content, spread misinformation, or even facilitate illegal activities.

For example, a language model trained with poisoned data might generate text that subtly promotes false narratives or harmful ideologies, thereby influencing public opinion or exacerbating social tensions.

Mitigating the risk of poisoning attacks requires a multifaceted approach. One strategy involves enhancing the robustness of the training process. Techniques such as data sanitization, where the training data is carefully inspected and cleaned, can help reduce the likelihood of incorporating malicious inputs. Additionally, employing robust learning algorithms that are less sensitive to outliers and anomalies can further protect against poisoning attempts.

Another critical defense mechanism is the use of anomaly detection systems. These systems are designed to identify and flag unusual patterns in the training data that might indicate the presence of poisoned inputs. By continuously monitoring the data pipeline, anomaly detection can provide an early warning system, allowing for timely intervention before the model is compromised.

Collaboration and information sharing among organizations can also play a vital role in combating poisoning attacks. By sharing knowledge about emerging threats and effective countermeasures, the community can collectively improve its defenses. Standardizing best practices and developing industry-wide guidelines can help ensure that all stakeholders are better prepared to detect and respond to these attacks.

The field of GenAI is rapidly evolving, and with it, the tactics employed by adversaries. Staying ahead of these threats requires ongoing research and innovation. By understanding the nature of poisoning attacks and implementing robust defensive measures, we can safeguard the integrity of GenAI systems and ensure that they continue to serve as powerful, trustworthy tools in our increasingly digital world.

Detection Methods

The increasing sophistication of Generative AI (GenAI) has not only revolutionized various industries but also opened the door to a myriad of malicious activities. Detecting and mitigating the misuse of these advanced technologies has become a critical area of focus. Various detection methods have been developed to identify and counteract the unethical applications of GenAI, ensuring that its benefits are not overshadowed by its potential for harm.

One of the primary detection methods involves the use of machine learning algorithms designed to recognize patterns indicative of AI-generated content. These algorithms analyze textual, visual, or audio data for characteristics that differentiate human-made creations from those produced by GenAI. For instance, in the realm of textual analysis, certain linguistic patterns, syntactic structures, and inconsistencies can signal the presence of AI-generated text. Similarly, in image and video analysis, machine learning models can detect anomalies in pixel patterns, lighting inconsistencies, and unnatural movements that are often missed by the human eye.

Another effective technique is watermarking, which embeds a hidden, identifiable signature within AI-generated content. This digital watermark can be detected through specialized software, allowing for the easy identification of content origin. Watermarking not only aids in tracing the source of the content but also acts as a deterrent against the misuse of GenAI. By making it easier to trace and attribute AI-generated content, watermarking helps maintain accountability and transparency.

In addition to watermarking, digital forensics plays a crucial role in detecting GenAI misuse. Forensic experts employ a range of tools and techniques to examine the metadata and digital footprints left behind by AI systems. This process involves scrutinizing the creation and modification timestamps, file properties, and other metadata that can reveal the involvement of GenAI in the content generation process. Digital forensics can also uncover evidence of tampering or manipulation, further aiding in the identification of malicious activities.

Behavioral analysis is another promising method for detecting GenAI misuse. By monitoring the behavior of users and systems, anomalies that suggest the involvement of GenAI can be identified. This approach involves tracking user interactions, access patterns, and system responses to detect deviations from normal behavior. For example, an unusually high volume of content generation or access requests may indicate the presence of automated GenAI systems. Behavioral analysis can be particularly effective in real-time detection, enabling swift intervention to prevent potential harm.

Collaboration between industry, academia, and government is essential for the development and implementation of effective detection methods. Sharing knowledge, resources, and best practices can enhance the collective ability to identify and mitigate GenAI misuse. Industry standards and regulatory frameworks can provide guidelines for the ethical use of GenAI, while academic research can drive innovation in detection technologies.

Government agencies can support these efforts through policy-making and enforcement, ensuring a coordinated and comprehensive approach to addressing the challenges posed by GenAI.

Public awareness and education also play a vital role in the detection and prevention of GenAI misuse. By informing individuals about the potential risks and signs of AI-generated content, a more vigilant and informed public can contribute to the early detection of malicious activities. Educational initiatives can empower users to recognize and report suspicious content, fostering a collaborative effort to combat the dark side of GenAI.

Detecting the misuse of GenAI requires a multifaceted approach that leverages advanced technologies, collaborative efforts, and public awareness. By employing a combination of machine learning algorithms, watermarking, digital forensics, and behavioral analysis, society can effectively identify and counteract the threats posed by unethical applications of GenAI. Through continued innovation and cooperation, the benefits of GenAI can be harnessed while minimizing its potential for harm.

Case Studies

The rapid development of Generative Artificial Intelligence (GenAI) has not only revolutionized industries but also exposed significant ethical and practical challenges. By examining specific instances where GenAI has been implemented, we can better understand the complexities and potential pitfalls associated with this technology.

One prominent example is the use of GenAI in the creation of deepfake videos. Initially celebrated for its potential in entertainment and media, deepfakes quickly became a tool for misinformation and manipulation. In 2020, a deepfake video of a prominent political figure went viral, falsely depicting them making controversial statements. The video was so convincingly realistic that it took experts several days to debunk it. During this time, the video had already influenced public opinion and caused significant damage to the individual's reputation. This case highlights the urgent need for robust verification mechanisms and ethical guidelines to prevent the misuse of GenAI.

Another case involves the application of GenAI in the healthcare sector. A biotech company developed an AI model capable of generating novel drug compounds. While the technology showed promise in accelerating drug discovery, it also raised concerns about the potential for creating harmful substances. In one instance, the AI inadvertently generated a compound with toxic properties. This incident underscored the necessity for stringent oversight and thorough testing to ensure that GenAI applications in sensitive fields like healthcare do not pose risks to human safety.

The advertising industry has also seen controversial uses of GenAI. A major retailer employed GenAI to create personalized marketing campaigns. The AI analyzed vast amounts of personal data to generate targeted advertisements. However, this led to significant privacy concerns. Customers began to feel uneasy about the extent of data being collected and the invasive nature of the personalized ads. The backlash prompted regulatory bodies to scrutinize the use of GenAI in marketing, leading to stricter data protection laws. This case illustrates the delicate balance between innovation and privacy, emphasizing the need for transparent data practices and consumer consent.

In the realm of creative arts, GenAI has been both a boon and a bane. A software company released an AI tool capable of generating music compositions. While some artists embraced the technology as a new creative partner, others saw it as a threat to their livelihood. One notable incident involved an AI-generated song that closely resembled a copyrighted piece. The ensuing legal battle raised questions about intellectual property rights and the originality of AI-generated content. This case demonstrates the complex intersection of creativity, ownership, and technology, calling for updated legal frameworks to address the unique challenges posed by GenAI.

The financial sector has also grappled with the implications of GenAI. An investment firm used AI algorithms to predict stock market trends and make trading decisions. Initially, the AI outperformed human analysts, leading to substantial profits. However, during a market downturn, the AI made a series of poor decisions, resulting in significant financial losses. This episode highlighted the limitations of relying solely on AI for high-stakes decision-making and the importance of human oversight. It also raised concerns about the transparency and accountability of AI-driven financial practices.

These case studies collectively underscore the dual-edged nature of GenAI. While the technology holds immense potential for innovation and efficiency, it also presents serious ethical and practical challenges. Each instance reveals the critical need for comprehensive regulatory frameworks, ethical guidelines, and ongoing dialogue among stakeholders to navigate the dark side of GenAI responsibly.

Impact Analysis

Generative Artificial Intelligence (GenAI) has revolutionized numerous sectors, from healthcare to entertainment, yet its darker aspects warrant a thorough examination. The analysis of its impact reveals an intricate web of both benefits and significant risks that society must navigate.

One of the most profound impacts of GenAI is its potential to disrupt the labor market. Automation powered by GenAI promises increased efficiency and reduced costs, but it also poses a threat to jobs that involve repetitive tasks. Workers in sectors such as manufacturing, customer service, and even some areas of healthcare may find their roles increasingly redundant. This shift necessitates a reevaluation of workforce development strategies, emphasizing the need for reskilling and upskilling programs. Without proactive measures, economic disparities could widen, leading to social unrest and increased unemployment rates.

Another critical area affected by GenAI is privacy. The ability of these systems to generate highly realistic text, images, and even videos raises concerns about data security and individual privacy. Deepfake technology, a product of GenAI, can create convincing but false representations of individuals, posing significant risks to personal reputations and public trust. The spread of misinformation and disinformation becomes easier, potentially influencing public opinion and even election outcomes. The challenge lies in developing robust regulatory frameworks and technological solutions to counteract these threats while balancing innovation and privacy.

Intellectual property rights also face challenges in the age of GenAI. The capacity of these systems to produce content that mimics human creativity blurs the lines of authorship and ownership. Artists, writers, and other content creators may find their work being replicated or modified without their consent, raising ethical and legal questions. Establishing clear guidelines on the use and ownership of AI-generated content is crucial to protect the interests of original creators and maintain the integrity of intellectual property laws.

Moreover, the ethical implications of GenAI's decision-making processes cannot be ignored. These systems often operate as black boxes, making it difficult to understand how they arrive at specific conclusions. This opacity can lead to biased outcomes, especially if the training data contains inherent biases. In fields such as law enforcement and healthcare, biased AI decisions can have severe consequences, perpetuating existing inequalities and injustices. There is an urgent need for transparency and accountability in the development and deployment of GenAI systems to ensure they serve all segments of society fairly.

Environmental considerations also come into play. The training and operation of GenAI models require substantial computational power, leading to significant energy consumption. As awareness of climate change grows, the environmental footprint of these technologies cannot be overlooked. Developing more energy-efficient algorithms and leveraging renewable energy sources are steps that can mitigate this impact.

The influence of GenAI extends to the realm of human interaction and mental health. The advent of AI-generated companions and chatbots raises questions about the nature of relationships and social connections. While these technologies can provide companionship and support, they may also lead to increased isolation and a decline in genuine human interactions. Understanding the psychological impact of these AI systems is essential to harness their benefits without compromising mental well-being.

In summary, the impact of GenAI is multifaceted, presenting both opportunities and challenges. Addressing the associated risks requires a collaborative effort from policymakers, technologists, and society at large. By fostering a balanced approach, it is possible to leverage the transformative potential of GenAI while mitigating its darker consequences.

7. Privacy Compromise and Data Exfiltration

Privacy Compromise Tactics

Generative AI (GenAI) has brought transformative capabilities to various sectors, but it also poses significant threats to personal privacy. One of the most alarming aspects of GenAI is its ability to compromise privacy through sophisticated tactics that exploit user data in unprecedented ways. Understanding these tactics is crucial for developing strategies to protect personal information.

One primary method by which GenAI compromises privacy is through data scraping and aggregation. By collecting vast amounts of data from various sources, GenAI systems can create comprehensive profiles of individuals. These profiles often include personal details, preferences, and behavioral patterns, which can be used to predict future actions or manipulate decision-making processes. Data scraping is not new, but GenAI's ability to process and analyze this data at scale makes it particularly invasive.

Another tactic involves the use of deepfake technology. Deepfakes are hyper-realistic digital manipulations created by GenAI, often used to impersonate individuals convincingly. These can range from fake videos and audio recordings to realistic text conversations. The potential for misuse is vast, from identity theft and fraud to damaging personal reputations. Deepfakes undermine trust in digital content, making it difficult to distinguish between genuine and manipulated information.

Phishing attacks have also evolved with the advent of GenAI. Traditional phishing attempts often involve generic messages that are relatively easy to identify. However, GenAI can craft highly personalized phishing messages by analyzing an individual's online behavior and communication style. These targeted attacks are much harder to detect and can lead to significant breaches of personal information.

Moreover, GenAI can be used to exploit vulnerabilities in social media platforms. By analyzing user interactions and identifying patterns, GenAI can predict and influence user behavior. This can be used to spread misinformation, manipulate opinions, or even incite harmful actions. The ability to influence large groups of people through tailored content raises ethical and security concerns that are difficult to address.

Another concerning tactic is the use of GenAI in surveillance. Advanced AI algorithms can process video feeds, social media activity, and other data streams to monitor individuals in real-time. This can be used by governments, corporations, or malicious actors to track movements, predict activities, and gather sensitive information without consent. The potential for abuse in surveillance is enormous, as it can lead to a significant loss of personal freedom and autonomy.

Additionally, GenAI can be used to de-anonymize data. Even when data is anonymized to protect user privacy, GenAI's advanced analytical capabilities can often re-identify individuals by correlating various data points. This poses a significant risk, as it undermines efforts to protect personal information through anonymization techniques.

The integration of GenAI into everyday applications also raises privacy concerns. Many consumer products and services now incorporate AI to enhance user experience. However, these systems often require access to personal data, creating potential vulnerabilities. For instance, smart home devices or virtual assistants collect and process data continuously, which can be exploited if not properly secured.

In essence, the tactics employed by GenAI to compromise privacy are multifaceted and continually evolving. The ability to collect, analyze, and manipulate data at unprecedented scales presents significant challenges. Addressing these issues requires a comprehensive understanding of how GenAI operates and the implementation of robust safeguards to protect personal information. The dark side of GenAI, therefore, lies not only in its capabilities but also in the ethical and security implications it brings.

Data Exfiltration Methods

Data exfiltration, the unauthorized transfer of data from a computer, is a critical concern in the realm of cybersecurity, especially in the context of Generative AI (GenAI). Cybercriminals employ various techniques to siphon off sensitive information, leveraging the capabilities of advanced AI to enhance their methods. Understanding these techniques is essential for developing robust defenses against such threats.

One prevalent method is the use of malware. Malicious software can be designed to infiltrate systems and exfiltrate data without detection. Advanced malware often employs encryption to mask its activities, making it difficult for traditional security measures to identify the breach. GenAI can be used to create sophisticated malware that adapts to security protocols, ensuring its persistence within the network.

Phishing remains a highly effective technique for data exfiltration. Cybercriminals craft convincing emails that trick recipients into divulging sensitive information or clicking on malicious links. With the aid of GenAI, these phishing attempts can be made even more convincing. AI can analyze vast amounts of data to personalize emails, increasing the likelihood of deceiving the target. Additionally, AI-generated deepfakes can create realistic audio or video messages, adding another layer of deception.

Insider threats are another significant vector for data exfiltration. Employees with legitimate access to sensitive data can be coerced, bribed, or manipulated into exfiltrating information. GenAI can assist in identifying potential insider threats by analyzing behavioral patterns and detecting anomalies. Conversely, malicious actors can use AI to manipulate insiders more effectively by crafting persuasive messages tailored to individual vulnerabilities.

Network traffic analysis is a technique employed by both attackers and defenders. Cybercriminals use AI to monitor network traffic, identifying patterns and vulnerabilities that can be exploited to exfiltrate data. AI can automate the process of scanning for open ports, weak encryption, and other potential entry points. On the defensive side, AI can analyze network traffic to detect unusual patterns indicative of data exfiltration attempts.

The use of external devices, such as USB drives, remains a straightforward yet effective method for data exfiltration. AI can be used to automate the detection of unauthorized devices connected to the network, alerting security teams to potential breaches. However, cybercriminals can also use AI to bypass these defenses, for example, by creating devices that mimic authorized ones or by using AI to predict and exploit periods of reduced network monitoring.

Steganography, the practice of hiding data within other data, is another method enhanced by GenAI. Cybercriminals can embed exfiltrated data within images, audio files, or other seemingly benign files. AI algorithms can automate the process of embedding and extracting hidden data, making it more efficient and harder to detect. Security teams must employ similarly advanced techniques to uncover these hidden threats.

Cloud services present both opportunities and risks for data exfiltration. While cloud providers offer robust security measures, they are also attractive targets for cybercriminals. AI can be used to automate the process of identifying and exploiting vulnerabilities within cloud environments. For instance, attackers can use AI to scan for misconfigured storage buckets or weak access controls. Conversely, AI can help cloud providers enhance their security by continuously monitoring for and responding to potential threats.

In the evolving landscape of cybersecurity, the interplay between GenAI and data exfiltration methods presents both challenges and opportunities. As cybercriminals continue to innovate, leveraging the capabilities of AI to enhance their tactics, defenders must also harness AI to anticipate, detect, and mitigate these threats effectively. Understanding the methods employed for data exfiltration is the first step in building a resilient defense against the dark side of GenAI.

Preventative Measures

The rapid evolution of Generative AI (GenAI) has brought forth remarkable advancements, but it has also exposed significant risks that require proactive management. To mitigate these risks, a multi-faceted approach involving technical, ethical, and regulatory measures is essential. Implementing robust preventative measures can help ensure that GenAI technologies are developed and deployed responsibly.

One critical aspect of prevention involves the development of stringent ethical guidelines. These guidelines should be established by collaborative efforts among AI researchers, ethicists, and policymakers. They must address issues such as bias, transparency, and accountability. By setting clear ethical standards, it becomes possible to create a framework within which GenAI can operate safely and fairly. For instance, guidelines can mandate the inclusion of diverse datasets to minimize biases and require transparency in the algorithms' decision-making processes.

Another key preventative measure is the implementation of rigorous testing and validation protocols. Before deploying GenAI systems, they should undergo extensive testing to identify and rectify potential vulnerabilities. This includes stress-testing the systems under various scenarios to ensure they perform reliably and securely. Regular audits and updates are also crucial to adapt to emerging threats and maintain the integrity of the systems. By continuously monitoring and improving GenAI, it is possible to prevent misuse and reduce the likelihood of unintended consequences.

Education and training play a vital role in preventing the misuse of GenAI. By educating developers, users, and the general public about the potential risks and ethical considerations, it becomes easier to foster a culture of responsibility. Training programs can equip developers with the skills needed to create secure and ethical GenAI applications. Additionally, raising awareness among users about the limitations and potential dangers of GenAI can help them make informed decisions and avoid contributing to harmful practices.

Regulatory oversight is another essential component of preventative measures. Governments and regulatory bodies must establish and enforce laws that govern the development and use of GenAI. These regulations should be designed to protect public interest while promoting innovation. For example, regulations can require companies to conduct impact assessments before releasing GenAI products and hold them accountable for any negative outcomes. By creating a legal framework, it is possible to deter malicious actors and ensure that GenAI technologies are used responsibly.

Collaboration between various stakeholders is crucial for the effective implementation of preventative measures. This includes partnerships between academic institutions, industry leaders, and government agencies. By sharing knowledge and resources, stakeholders can develop comprehensive strategies to address the risks associated with GenAI. International cooperation is also important, as the global nature of AI development means that risks and solutions are not confined to any single country. Collaborative efforts can lead to the creation of universal standards and best practices that benefit everyone.

Investing in research and development to advance the safety and robustness of GenAI systems is another preventative measure. By prioritizing research focused on enhancing the security and reliability of these technologies, it is possible to stay ahead of potential threats. This includes exploring new techniques for detecting and mitigating biases, improving the interpretability of AI models, and developing fail-safe mechanisms to prevent catastrophic failures. Continuous innovation in these areas can help build more resilient GenAI systems that are better equipped to handle unforeseen challenges.

Preventative measures are essential to harness the potential of GenAI while safeguarding against its dark side. By establishing ethical guidelines, implementing rigorous testing protocols, educating stakeholders, enforcing regulatory oversight, fostering collaboration, and investing in research, it is possible to create a safer and more responsible GenAI landscape.

Regulatory Frameworks

The rapid evolution of generative artificial intelligence (GenAI) has outpaced the development of comprehensive regulatory frameworks. This discrepancy presents a significant challenge, as the potential for misuse and unintended consequences becomes increasingly apparent. Governments and international bodies are now grappling with the need to establish guidelines that can effectively balance innovation with safety and ethical considerations.

One of the primary concerns in regulating GenAI is the technology's inherent capacity for generating highly realistic content. This includes everything from deepfakes, which can be used to spread misinformation, to sophisticated text generation that could facilitate cybercrimes or manipulate public opinion. To address these risks, policymakers are attempting to craft regulations that specifically target the misuse of GenAI while still allowing for its beneficial applications in fields such as healthcare, education, and creative industries.

Several countries have already taken steps to impose restrictions on certain uses of GenAI. For example, the European Union has proposed the Artificial Intelligence Act, which categorizes AI applications into different levels of risk and mandates corresponding levels of regulatory scrutiny. High-risk applications, such as those in critical infrastructure or law enforcement, would be subject to stringent requirements, including transparency, accountability, and human oversight. This tiered approach aims to mitigate the most severe risks while not stifling innovation in lower-risk areas.

In contrast, the United States has adopted a more decentralized strategy, with various federal and state agencies issuing their own guidelines and regulations. This patchwork approach has led to inconsistencies and gaps in oversight, prompting calls for more cohesive national policies. Some experts advocate for the establishment of a dedicated federal agency to oversee AI technologies, akin to the Food and Drug Administration's role in regulating pharmaceuticals and medical devices. Such an agency could standardize regulations, conduct impact assessments, and enforce compliance, thereby providing a more unified framework for GenAI governance.

International cooperation is also crucial, given the global nature of AI development and deployment. Organizations like the United Nations and the Organisation for Economic Co-operation and Development (OECD) are working towards creating international standards and best practices for AI governance. These efforts aim to foster collaboration among nations, ensuring that regulations are harmonized to prevent regulatory arbitrage, where companies might relocate to jurisdictions with more lenient rules.

Ethical considerations are at the forefront of the regulatory discourse. Issues such as bias, privacy, and accountability need to be addressed to ensure that GenAI systems are fair and trustworthy. For instance, algorithms trained on biased data can perpetuate and even exacerbate social inequalities. Regulatory frameworks must include provisions for auditing AI systems for bias and ensuring that developers implement corrective measures when necessary.

Privacy concerns are equally pressing, especially with GenAI's ability to generate detailed personal information. Regulations like the General Data

Protection Regulation (GDPR) in the EU set a precedent for data protection, emphasizing the need for explicit consent and transparency in data usage. Extending these principles to GenAI technologies can help safeguard individual privacy while still enabling the technology's positive applications.

Accountability is another critical aspect. Clear guidelines on liability are necessary to determine who is responsible when GenAI systems cause harm or produce harmful content. This could involve holding developers, deployers, and even users accountable, depending on the context and the nature of the harm caused.

As GenAI continues to advance, regulatory frameworks must evolve in tandem. This dynamic landscape requires ongoing dialogue between technologists, policymakers, ethicists, and the public to ensure that the benefits of GenAI are realized while minimizing its darker potentials.

Future Challenges

Generative Artificial Intelligence (GenAI) has revolutionized numerous sectors, from creative industries to healthcare, offering unprecedented possibilities. However, as with any transformative technology, it brings a host of future challenges that need careful consideration and proactive management. One significant concern is the ethical implications surrounding GenAI's capabilities. These systems can generate highly realistic text, images, and even deepfakes, which can be misused to spread misinformation, manipulate public opinion, and compromise privacy. Ensuring that GenAI is used responsibly while safeguarding against its potential for harm is a complex task that requires robust regulatory frameworks and continuous oversight.

Another pressing issue is the impact on employment. GenAI's ability to automate tasks traditionally performed by humans raises questions about job displacement and economic inequality. While some argue that GenAI will create new job opportunities, the transition may not be smooth for everyone. Workers in industries heavily affected by automation may face significant challenges in adapting to new roles, necessitating comprehensive re-skilling and up-skilling programs. Policymakers, educators, and industry leaders must collaborate to develop strategies that mitigate these impacts and support a more inclusive workforce.

Data privacy is another critical challenge. GenAI systems require vast amounts of data to function effectively, often sourced from users' personal information. This raises concerns about how data is collected, stored, and used. Ensuring that GenAI systems adhere to stringent data protection standards is essential to maintain public trust and prevent misuse. Moreover, as these systems become more integrated into daily life, the potential for data breaches and unauthorized access increases, necessitating advanced security measures and transparent data governance policies.

The environmental impact of GenAI cannot be overlooked. Training and deploying these systems require substantial computational resources, leading to significant energy consumption and carbon emissions. As the demand for GenAI applications grows, so does its environmental footprint. Researchers and developers must prioritize the creation of more energy-efficient algorithms and explore sustainable practices to minimize this impact. Balancing the benefits of GenAI with its ecological consequences is crucial for sustainable technological progress.

Bias and fairness in GenAI models present another formidable challenge. These systems learn from existing data, which can contain inherent biases, leading to biased outputs. Addressing this issue involves not only refining the algorithms but also critically examining and curating the training data. Ensuring fairness and reducing bias in GenAI is vital for creating equitable systems that serve all users without perpetuating existing societal inequalities. Continuous research and collaborative efforts are required to develop methodologies that identify and mitigate biases in these complex models.

The rapid advancement of GenAI also poses challenges in terms of regulation and governance. The pace at which technology evolves often outstrips the development of appropriate legal and ethical guidelines. Establishing comprehensive regulations that keep up with the technological advancements while fostering innovation is a delicate balance. International cooperation and dialogue are essential to create a cohesive framework that addresses the global implications of GenAI.

In addressing these future challenges, a multi-faceted approach is necessary. Collaboration between technologists, ethicists, policymakers, and the public will be crucial to navigate the complexities of GenAI. By anticipating potential issues and proactively seeking solutions, society can harness the benefits of GenAI while mitigating its risks, paving the way for responsible and sustainable technological advancement.

8. Human Likeness Manipulation

Techniques of Manipulation

Generative Artificial Intelligence (GenAI) has rapidly advanced, offering unprecedented capabilities in generating human-like text, images, and even audio. While these advancements hold the potential for positive applications, there exists a darker aspect that warrants careful examination. One of the critical concerns is the array of manipulation techniques that can be employed using GenAI. These techniques can be exploited to deceive, influence, and control individuals and societies, raising ethical and societal questions.

A prominent technique involves the creation of deepfakes, where AI-generated content is used to produce realistic but fake images and videos. These can be manipulated to show people saying or doing things they never did. The potential for harm is significant, ranging from personal reputations being tarnished to political instability. For instance, a deepfake video of a political leader making controversial statements could incite unrest or manipulate public opinion.

Another manipulation method is the generation of misleading textual content. GenAI can produce convincing fake news articles or social media posts. These fabricated narratives can be disseminated rapidly, influencing public discourse and decision-making processes. The ability to generate large volumes of content quickly makes it challenging to distinguish between genuine and fake information, thereby exacerbating the spread of misinformation.

Social engineering is another domain where GenAI can be weaponized. By analyzing vast amounts of data, AI can craft highly personalized messages that exploit individual psychological traits. These tailored messages can be used in phishing attacks, where individuals are tricked into revealing sensitive information. The sophistication of these AI-generated messages makes them more convincing, increasing the likelihood of successful attacks.

AI-driven chatbots represent another tool for manipulation. These chatbots can engage users in conversations that seem authentic, guiding them toward specific opinions or actions. In customer service or social media contexts, these interactions can be subtle yet effective in shaping perceptions and behaviors. The challenge lies in the difficulty of identifying whether one is interacting with a human or an AI, blurring the lines of authenticity.

Moreover, GenAI can be used to amplify echo chambers and filter bubbles. By analyzing user behavior and preferences, AI can generate content that reinforces existing beliefs and biases. This selective exposure can polarize communities, making it harder to achieve consensus or understand differing viewpoints. The reinforcement of biases through AI-generated content can deepen societal divisions and hinder constructive dialogue.

The manipulation of public sentiment is another critical area. GenAI can analyze social media trends and generate content that taps into prevailing emotions. By amplifying anger, fear, or excitement, AI can steer public sentiment in desired directions. This capability can be exploited in political campaigns, marketing strategies, or even to incite social movements.

These manipulation techniques underscore the need for robust ethical guidelines and regulatory frameworks. While GenAI holds immense promise, its potential for misuse cannot be overlooked. Addressing these challenges requires a multi-faceted approach, involving technological safeguards, public awareness, and policy interventions. The dark side of GenAI presents a formidable challenge, but understanding the techniques of manipulation is a crucial step toward mitigating their impact.

Real-World Examples

The impact of Generative AI (GenAI) is not confined to theoretical discussions or speculative scenarios. It has already made its presence felt in various sectors, often with alarming consequences. One notable instance is the proliferation of deepfake technology. Deepfakes utilize GenAI to create hyper-realistic videos and audio recordings that can convincingly mimic real people. This technology has been exploited for malicious purposes, including the creation of fake news, political propaganda, and even blackmail. In 2019, a deepfake video of a prominent public figure went viral, causing widespread misinformation and panic. The video was later debunked, but the damage had already been done, highlighting the potential for GenAI to erode trust in digital media.

Another concerning example is the use of GenAI in cybercrime. Cybercriminals have harnessed the power of AI to develop sophisticated phishing schemes and malware. In one high-profile case, a European energy company fell victim to a scam where the fraudsters used an AI-generated voice to impersonate the CEO and request a fraudulent transfer of $243,000. The employees, convinced they were following legitimate orders, complied, resulting in significant financial loss. This incident underscores the growing threat that GenAI poses to organizational security and the urgent need for robust countermeasures.

The advertising industry has also felt the disruptive force of GenAI. Companies are increasingly using AI-generated content to create personalized advertisements. While this can enhance user engagement, it also raises ethical questions. In an infamous case, a major tech company used GenAI to create targeted ads that exploited users' emotional vulnerabilities. The AI analyzed users' online behavior and generated ads that preyed on their insecurities, leading to widespread criticism and calls for stricter regulations. This example illustrates the fine line between innovation and exploitation in the realm of GenAI.

In the realm of social media, GenAI has been employed to generate fake profiles and manipulate public opinion. During the 2020 U.S. presidential election, thousands of AI-generated bots flooded social media platforms, spreading misinformation and polarizing public discourse. These bots were designed to mimic human behavior, making it difficult for users to distinguish between genuine and artificial interactions. The incident not only influenced the electoral process but also highlighted the potential for GenAI to undermine democratic institutions.

The healthcare sector is not immune to the dark side of GenAI either. While AI holds promise for medical advancements, it has also been used unethically. In one disturbing case, a pharmaceutical company employed GenAI to design a drug that could be weaponized. The AI-generated formula was initially intended for therapeutic purposes but was manipulated to create a toxic compound. This revelation raised serious concerns about the dual-use nature of GenAI and the need for stringent oversight.

These real-world examples demonstrate that the dark side of GenAI is not a distant threat but a present reality. The technology's potential for misuse spans various domains, from media and cybersecurity to advertising and healthcare. Each instance serves as a cautionary tale, urging stakeholders to consider the ethical implications and develop safeguards to mitigate the risks associated with GenAI.

Ethical Implications

The rise of Generative Artificial Intelligence (GenAI) has brought forth a multitude of opportunities, but it also presents significant ethical challenges. These challenges are multifaceted and demand careful consideration. The primary concern revolves around the potential for misuse. GenAI systems, with their ability to generate human-like text and images, can be weaponized to create deepfakes, misinformation, and propaganda. This capability poses a threat to the integrity of information and the trustworthiness of digital content.

One critical ethical issue is the potential for bias in GenAI models. These systems are trained on vast datasets that often contain biases present in the real world. As a result, the outputs generated by these models can inadvertently perpetuate and amplify existing prejudices. This raises questions about fairness and equity, particularly when GenAI is used in sensitive applications such as hiring, law enforcement, and healthcare. Ensuring that these systems do not reinforce societal biases is a complex challenge that requires ongoing vigilance and intervention.

Privacy is another significant concern. GenAI systems often rely on large amounts of personal data to function effectively. The collection, storage, and processing of this data raise questions about consent and the potential for abuse. There is a risk that individuals' privacy could be compromised, either through deliberate exploitation or unintentional data breaches. This concern is heightened by the fact that many users may not fully understand the extent to which their data is being used and the potential implications of this usage.

The accountability of GenAI systems is another pressing ethical issue. When these systems make decisions or generate content, determining who is responsible for the outcomes can be challenging. This lack of clear accountability can lead to situations where harmful consequences are not adequately addressed, and those affected may have little recourse.

Establishing mechanisms for accountability is crucial to ensure that the deployment of GenAI is done responsibly and that there is a clear path for addressing any negative impacts.

Transparency is closely related to accountability. The inner workings of GenAI systems are often opaque, even to their creators. This lack of transparency can make it difficult to understand how decisions are made and to identify potential sources of bias or error. Efforts to improve the explainability of these systems are essential to build trust and ensure that they are used ethically. Users need to have confidence that GenAI systems are operating in a fair and just manner.

The ethical implications of GenAI also extend to the broader societal impacts. As these systems become more prevalent, there is a risk of exacerbating existing inequalities. For example, the automation of certain jobs through GenAI could lead to significant economic displacement, disproportionately affecting vulnerable populations. Addressing these broader implications requires a holistic approach that considers the societal context in which GenAI is deployed and seeks to mitigate any negative consequences.

Ethical considerations in the development and deployment of GenAI are not just theoretical concerns; they have real-world implications that affect individuals and society as a whole. It is imperative that stakeholders, including developers, policymakers, and the public, engage in ongoing dialogue to navigate these challenges. By proactively addressing the ethical implications of GenAI, it is possible to harness its potential for good while minimizing the risks and ensuring that its benefits are equitably distributed.

Psychological Impact

Generative Artificial Intelligence (GenAI) has revolutionized numerous aspects of our daily lives, from automating mundane tasks to creating art. However, the psychological impact of this technology remains an area of growing concern. As GenAI systems become more integrated into society, they bring with them a range of psychological effects that are only beginning to be understood.

One of the most significant psychological effects of GenAI is the potential for increased feelings of isolation and loneliness. As people increasingly rely on AI for companionship and interaction, there is a risk that human relationships will suffer. While AI companions can provide a semblance of social interaction, they lack the depth and emotional complexity that human relationships offer. This can lead to a paradox where individuals are surrounded by AI entities but feel more isolated than ever.

Another critical issue is the erosion of self-efficacy. GenAI systems are designed to perform tasks that traditionally required human effort and skill. While this can enhance productivity, it can also diminish individuals' sense of accomplishment and self-worth. When an AI can effortlessly create a piece of art or solve a complex problem, people may feel their own efforts are less valuable. This can lead to a decline in motivation and a sense of purposelessness.

The impact on mental health cannot be overlooked. The ubiquitous presence of GenAI can contribute to heightened levels of anxiety and stress. The rapid pace of technological change and the pressure to keep up with AI advancements can create a constant sense of unease. Moreover, the reliance on AI for decision-making can lead to a diminished sense of control over one's life, further exacerbating stress and anxiety.

GenAI also raises ethical concerns that can have psychological repercussions. The use of AI in surveillance and data collection can lead to feelings of paranoia and distrust. Knowing that one's actions and communications are constantly monitored by AI systems can create a pervasive sense of being watched, which can be mentally exhausting and lead to a breakdown in social trust.

Furthermore, the advent of GenAI has implications for identity formation. As AI systems become more adept at mimicking human behaviors and characteristics, the lines between human and machine become blurred. This can lead to an identity crisis, where individuals struggle to define what it means to be human in an age of intelligent machines. The challenge of distinguishing oneself from AI can create existential angst and a profound sense of disorientation.

The influence of GenAI on creativity and originality is another area of concern. While AI can generate creative content, it often does so by mimicking existing patterns and styles. This can lead to a homogenization of culture, where unique and original ideas are overshadowed by AI-generated content. For creative professionals, this can be particularly disheartening, as it may feel like their unique contributions are being drowned out by a sea of AI-generated material.

Lastly, the dependency on GenAI can lead to a decrease in critical thinking skills. When AI systems are used to provide answers and solutions, there is less incentive for individuals to engage in deep, analytical thinking. This can result in a population that is less capable of critical reasoning and problem-solving, which are essential skills for personal and societal growth.

In exploring the psychological impact of GenAI, it becomes clear that while the technology offers numerous benefits, it also presents significant challenges that must be addressed. Understanding these psychological effects is crucial for developing strategies to mitigate the negative impacts and ensure that GenAI is used in a way that enhances, rather than diminishes, human well-being.

Mitigation Strategies

Mitigating the challenges posed by Generative Artificial Intelligence (GenAI) requires a multifaceted approach, integrating technological, ethical, and regulatory strategies. The complexity of GenAI necessitates a robust framework to address potential misuse, biases, and the broader societal impacts. Developing effective mitigation strategies begins with understanding the inherent risks and implementing measures to counteract them.

One critical area of focus is the development of robust and transparent algorithms. Ensuring that GenAI systems are designed with fairness and accountability in mind can help mitigate biases that may arise from the data they are trained on. This involves adopting practices such as regular audits, bias detection tools, and transparency in the algorithmic decision-making process. Researchers and developers should prioritize creating systems that not only perform efficiently but also uphold ethical standards.

Another important strategy is the establishment of comprehensive regulatory frameworks. Governments and regulatory bodies need to collaborate with technologists and ethicists to create guidelines that govern the use of GenAI. These regulations should address issues such as data privacy, consent, and the ethical use of AI-generated content. By setting clear boundaries and enforcing compliance, it is possible to prevent malicious uses of GenAI, such as deepfakes, misinformation, and other forms of digital deception.

Educational initiatives also play a vital role in mitigating the risks associated with GenAI. Raising awareness about the capabilities and limitations of GenAI among the general public, as well as within specific industries, can help foster a more informed and critical approach to AI-generated content. Educational programs should aim to equip individuals with the skills to discern and critically evaluate information, thereby reducing the susceptibility to manipulation and misinformation.

Collaboration between various stakeholders is essential in the development and implementation of effective mitigation strategies. This includes partnerships between academia, industry, government, and civil society organizations. By working together, these groups can share knowledge, resources, and best practices, leading to more comprehensive and effective solutions. For example, interdisciplinary research can provide insights into the social and psychological impacts of GenAI, informing the development of more holistic mitigation measures.

The role of continuous monitoring and evaluation cannot be overstated. Implementing systems for ongoing assessment of GenAI applications allows for the identification of new risks and the effectiveness of existing mitigation strategies. This adaptive approach ensures that measures can be updated and refined in response to emerging challenges. Feedback loops involving stakeholders at all levels can enhance the responsiveness and resilience of mitigation efforts.

Investing in technological advancements that enhance the security and integrity of GenAI systems is another crucial strategy. This includes the development of advanced encryption methods, secure data storage solutions, and techniques for verifying the authenticity of AI-generated content. By strengthening the technical safeguards around GenAI, it is possible to reduce the likelihood of exploitation and misuse.

Ethical guidelines and standards should be integral to the development and deployment of GenAI. Organizations and developers should adhere to principles that prioritize human well-being, fairness, and transparency. Establishing ethical review boards and incorporating ethical considerations into the design and deployment phases can help ensure that GenAI technologies are used responsibly.

Addressing the dark side of GenAI is a complex and ongoing challenge. By combining technological innovation, regulatory oversight, educational efforts, and collaborative initiatives, it is possible to develop effective mitigation strategies that minimize risks and maximize the benefits of this powerful technology.

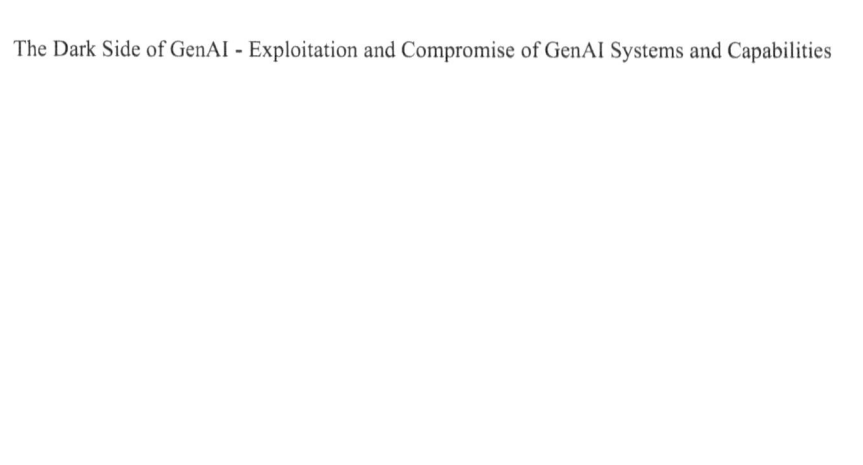

9. Opinion Manipulation and Disinformation

Strategies for Opinion Manipulation

Generative Artificial Intelligence (GenAI) has revolutionized various domains, including content creation, data analysis, and customer service. However, its capabilities also present significant risks, particularly in the realm of opinion manipulation. The sophisticated algorithms that power GenAI can be harnessed to subtly and effectively shape public perception and opinion, often without the awareness of the individuals being influenced.

One of the primary methods used in opinion manipulation is the creation of persuasive and tailored content. GenAI systems analyze vast amounts of data, including social media posts, search histories, and online interactions, to understand individual preferences and biases. Armed with this information, these systems can generate customized content that resonates with specific audiences. This tailored content can take the form of articles, social media posts, videos, or even comments, all designed to nudge individuals towards a particular viewpoint.

Another strategy involves the amplification of certain narratives while suppressing others. GenAI can be employed to flood social media platforms and news outlets with specific messages, creating an illusion of widespread consensus. This can be particularly effective in polarizing topics where the aim is to sway public opinion by making one side appear more popular or credible. By controlling the visibility and frequency of certain narratives, opinion manipulators can significantly influence the perceived legitimacy of different viewpoints.

Moreover, GenAI can be used to create deepfakes and other forms of synthetic media. These sophisticated forgeries can depict public figures making statements or engaging in actions that never occurred. The realistic nature of these deepfakes makes them a powerful tool for discrediting opponents, spreading misinformation, or rallying support for a cause. Once disseminated, these deepfakes can go viral, reaching a vast audience before they are debunked, if they are ever debunked at all.

The use of bots and automated accounts also plays a crucial role in opinion manipulation. GenAI-powered bots can simulate human behavior, engaging in discussions, liking posts, and sharing content to create an artificial sense of popularity or controversy. These bots can operate at a scale and speed that is impossible for humans, making them incredibly effective at steering online conversations and shaping public sentiment.

Sentiment analysis and predictive analytics further enhance the ability of GenAI to manipulate opinions. By continuously monitoring public sentiment, these systems can adapt their strategies in real-time, ensuring that the content remains relevant and persuasive. Predictive analytics can also identify emerging trends and potential shifts in public opinion, allowing manipulators to pre-emptively address or exploit these changes.

In addition to these direct methods, GenAI can also subtly influence opinions through more indirect means. For instance, recommendation algorithms that prioritize certain types of content can shape the information diet of users, gradually steering their beliefs and attitudes. Over time, this can lead to significant shifts in public opinion without any overt manipulation.

The potential for GenAI to manipulate opinions raises important ethical and regulatory questions. As these technologies continue to evolve, it is crucial to develop safeguards and oversight mechanisms to prevent their misuse. Public awareness and critical thinking are also essential in mitigating the impact of these manipulative strategies. Understanding how GenAI can be used to influence opinions is the first step in addressing the challenges posed by this powerful technology.

Disinformation Campaigns

Generative Artificial Intelligence (GenAI) has introduced transformative advancements across various sectors, but it also has a darker side that warrants critical examination. One particularly concerning aspect is the use of GenAI in disinformation campaigns. These campaigns can manipulate public opinion, disrupt democratic processes, and even incite violence.

Disinformation campaigns leverage GenAI to create and disseminate false information at an unprecedented scale and speed. Unlike traditional methods of spreading misinformation, GenAI can produce highly convincing fake news articles, deepfake videos, and synthetic social media posts that are difficult to distinguish from authentic content. This capability poses a significant threat to the integrity of information ecosystems and the public's ability to discern truth from falsehood.

The ease with which GenAI can generate content has lowered the barriers for malicious actors to engage in disinformation. Automated bots powered by GenAI can flood social media platforms with misleading information, creating an illusion of widespread consensus or dissent. These bots can interact with real users, amplifying false narratives and sowing confusion. The rapid spread of disinformation can undermine trust in institutions, erode social cohesion, and destabilize societies.

One of the most insidious aspects of GenAI-driven disinformation is its ability to target specific individuals or groups with tailored content. By analyzing vast amounts of data, GenAI can identify vulnerabilities and craft messages that exploit these weaknesses. For example, during election cycles, disinformation campaigns can target undecided voters with customized propaganda designed to sway their opinions. This micro-targeting capability makes disinformation efforts more effective and harder to counter.

The use of deepfake technology in disinformation campaigns is particularly alarming. Deepfakes are hyper-realistic digital manipulations of audio and video that can make it appear as though individuals are saying or doing things they never did. These fabrications can be used to discredit public figures, spread false information, or incite violence. The potential for deepfakes to cause real-world harm is immense, as they can erode trust in visual and auditory evidence, which has traditionally been considered reliable.

Combatting GenAI-driven disinformation requires a multi-faceted approach. Technological solutions, such as advanced detection algorithms, can help identify and flag disinformation. However, these tools are in a constant race against ever-evolving GenAI capabilities. Policy interventions, including regulations and international agreements, are necessary to establish norms and hold perpetrators accountable. Additionally, public awareness and education are crucial in building resilience against disinformation. Citizens need to be equipped with critical thinking skills and digital literacy to navigate the complex information landscape.

Moreover, collaboration between technology companies, governments, and civil society is essential. Tech companies have a responsibility to implement robust measures to detect and mitigate disinformation on their platforms. Governments must balance the need for regulation with the protection of free speech. Civil society organizations can play a key role in monitoring disinformation and advocating for transparency and accountability.

The ethical implications of GenAI in disinformation campaigns cannot be overstated. As the technology continues to evolve, so too will the challenges it presents. Addressing these challenges requires a concerted effort to understand the capabilities and limitations of GenAI, develop effective countermeasures, and foster an informed and resilient public. The stakes are high, and the consequences of inaction could be profound, affecting the very fabric of democratic societies and the trust that underpins them.

Case Studies

The deployment of Generative Artificial Intelligence (GenAI) has yielded both groundbreaking innovations and alarming ethical quandaries. Examining specific instances where GenAI has been utilized reveals the multifaceted impacts of this technology on society.

One notable case involves the use of GenAI in the creation of synthetic media, often referred to as deepfakes. In 2018, a deepfake video featuring a fabricated speech by former President Barack Obama surfaced, raising public awareness about the potential for misinformation. This video, generated by sophisticated algorithms, demonstrated how GenAI could be exploited to manipulate public opinion and erode trust in digital content. The implications are profound, as the technology can be used to create convincing yet entirely fabricated video and audio recordings. This case underscores the urgent need for robust detection methods and ethical guidelines to govern the use of GenAI in media.

In another instance, the application of GenAI in automated content generation has sparked debates within the creative industries. In 2020,

OpenAI's GPT-3 model was released, showcasing its ability to generate human-like text based on minimal input. While this technology holds promise for enhancing productivity and creativity, it also raises concerns about authorship and originality. A notable example is the use of GPT-3 to write articles and even short stories. Critics argue that relying on GenAI for creative writing could diminish the value of human creativity and lead to a homogenization of content. Moreover, the potential for intellectual property disputes arises when AI-generated content closely resembles existing works.

The healthcare sector has also witnessed the dual-edged nature of GenAI. In 2019, researchers developed an AI model capable of generating potential drug candidates. This breakthrough accelerated the drug discovery process, offering hope for faster development of treatments. However, the same technology also presents risks, such as the potential for generating harmful compounds if misused. The case of Insilico Medicine, a biotechnology company, highlights these concerns. Their AI system was able to generate thousands of potential drug molecules, but the ethical dilemma lies in the possibility of these models being repurposed for malicious intent, such as creating biochemical weapons.

Another significant case involves the use of GenAI in predictive policing. In several cities, law enforcement agencies have adopted AI systems to predict crime hotspots and allocate resources accordingly. While these systems aim to enhance public safety, they have been criticized for perpetuating biases present in historical crime data. A notable example is the deployment of such systems in Chicago, where critics argue that the technology disproportionately targets minority communities. This case illustrates the ethical challenges of using GenAI in decision-making processes that impact human lives and civil liberties.

The financial sector provides yet another example of GenAI's complex impact. High-frequency trading algorithms, powered by GenAI, have revolutionized stock markets by executing trades at unprecedented speeds. However, this technology has also contributed to market volatility and raised concerns about fairness. The 2010 "Flash Crash," where the Dow Jones Industrial Average plummeted and recovered within minutes, was partially attributed to algorithmic trading. This incident highlights the potential for GenAI to destabilize financial systems and the need for regulatory oversight.

These case studies exemplify the diverse and profound effects of GenAI across different domains. They highlight the necessity for a balanced approach that harnesses the benefits of this technology while addressing its ethical and societal challenges.

Impact on Public Discourse

Public discourse has undergone a significant transformation with the advent of Generative Artificial Intelligence (GenAI). This technology, capable of producing human-like text, images, and even audio, has both enriched and complicated the landscape of public communication. One of the most notable impacts of GenAI on public discourse is the amplification of misinformation. The ability to generate convincing but false narratives at scale poses a serious threat to the integrity of information. This has led to a proliferation of fake news, deepfakes, and other forms of digital deception that can mislead the public and undermine trust in media sources.

Another critical aspect is the erosion of accountability. Traditional forms of media and public communication are typically bound by ethical guidelines and professional standards. However, GenAI-generated content often lacks clear authorship, making it difficult to hold any entity accountable for misleading or harmful information. This anonymity can be exploited to spread propaganda, manipulate public opinion, and even incite violence without facing direct repercussions.

The democratization of content creation is another double-edged sword introduced by GenAI. On one hand, it empowers individuals to express themselves creatively and share their ideas with a broader audience. On the other hand, it also enables the spread of low-quality, sensationalist, or extremist content. The sheer volume of information generated can overwhelm traditional filtering mechanisms, making it challenging for consumers to discern credible sources from unreliable ones.

The role of social media platforms has also been significantly influenced by GenAI. Algorithms designed to maximize user engagement often prioritize sensational or emotionally charged content, which can be easily produced by GenAI. This has the effect of polarizing public discourse, as people are more likely to engage with content that confirms their biases or provokes strong emotional reactions. The echo chambers created by these algorithms can deepen societal divisions and reduce the likelihood of constructive dialogue.

Moreover, the ethical implications of GenAI in public discourse cannot be ignored. The technology's ability to mimic human communication raises questions about authenticity and consent. For instance, deepfake technology can create realistic but fabricated videos of public figures, leading to potential character assassination or blackmail. The lack of transparency in how GenAI-generated content is created and disseminated further complicates these ethical concerns.

The educational sector is also affected by GenAI's impact on public discourse. Students and educators alike face new challenges in distinguishing between authentic and artificially generated content. Critical thinking and media literacy have become more crucial than ever, as traditional methods of verifying information may no longer be sufficient. The need for updated curricula that address these challenges is becoming increasingly apparent.

Regulatory bodies and policymakers are grappling with how to manage the influence of GenAI on public discourse. Existing laws and regulations often lag behind technological advancements, making it difficult to address the unique challenges posed by GenAI. There is a growing consensus on the need for new frameworks that can effectively govern the use of this technology without stifling innovation.

In sum, the impact of Generative Artificial Intelligence on public discourse is profound and multifaceted. While it offers new avenues for creativity and expression, it also introduces significant risks that must be carefully managed. The balance between leveraging the benefits of GenAI and mitigating its potential harms will be a defining challenge for society in the coming years.

Countermeasures

Addressing the potential perils posed by Generative AI (GenAI) necessitates a multi-faceted approach encompassing technological, regulatory, and societal dimensions. The rapid advancement of GenAI technologies brings about transformative benefits, but it also introduces significant risks, including misinformation, privacy breaches, and ethical dilemmas. Countermeasures must be systematically designed and implemented to mitigate these risks effectively.

One of the primary technological countermeasures involves the development of robust detection systems to identify and flag AI-generated content. These systems utilize advanced machine learning algorithms capable of distinguishing between human-generated and AI-generated text, images, or videos. By leveraging large datasets and continuous learning, detection mechanisms can become increasingly accurate, thereby reducing the spread of misleading or harmful AI-generated material. Companies like OpenAI and Google are already investing in research to develop such detection tools, aiming to stay ahead of malicious actors who exploit GenAI capabilities.

Regulatory frameworks also play a crucial role in mitigating the risks associated with GenAI. Governments and international bodies must collaborate to establish clear guidelines and standards for the development and deployment of GenAI technologies. These regulations should encompass data privacy, ethical use, and accountability measures for AI developers and users. For instance, the European Union's General Data Protection Regulation (GDPR) provides a robust foundation for data privacy, which can be extended to address the specific challenges posed by

GenAI. Additionally, regulatory bodies should mandate transparency in AI systems, requiring developers to disclose the use of AI in content creation and the underlying data sources.

Ethical considerations are paramount in countering the dark side of GenAI. AI developers and researchers must adhere to ethical guidelines that prioritize human well-being and societal good. Implementing ethical AI principles, such as fairness, accountability, and transparency, can help ensure that GenAI technologies are developed and used responsibly. Organizations like the Partnership on AI and the IEEE Global Initiative on Ethics of Autonomous and Intelligent Systems provide valuable frameworks and resources to guide ethical AI development.

Public awareness and education are also critical components of an effective countermeasure strategy. By educating the public about the capabilities and limitations of GenAI, individuals can become more discerning consumers of digital content. Educational initiatives should focus on digital literacy, critical thinking, and the ability to identify AI-generated content. Schools, universities, and online platforms can play a significant role in disseminating this knowledge, thereby empowering individuals to navigate the digital landscape more safely.

Collaboration between various stakeholders, including tech companies, governments, academia, and civil society, is essential to tackle the challenges posed by GenAI. Joint efforts can lead to the development of comprehensive strategies and innovative solutions that address the multifaceted nature of GenAI risks. For example, public-private partnerships can foster the sharing of best practices, resources, and expertise, enhancing the overall efficacy of countermeasures.

Investment in continuous research and development is imperative to stay ahead of the evolving GenAI landscape. As AI technologies advance, so too must the tools and strategies designed to mitigate their risks. Ongoing research into AI ethics, security, and detection methods will provide the foundation for effective countermeasures. Funding and support for interdisciplinary research initiatives can drive innovation and ensure that countermeasures keep pace with the rapid evolution of GenAI.

In conclusion, mitigating the risks associated with GenAI requires a concerted effort across technological, regulatory, ethical, and educational domains. By implementing robust detection systems, establishing clear regulatory frameworks, adhering to ethical guidelines, raising public awareness, fostering collaboration, and investing in continuous research, society can harness the benefits of GenAI while minimizing its potential harms.

10. Monetization and Scams

Monetization Tactics

Generative Artificial Intelligence (GenAI) has revolutionized numerous industries, offering unprecedented capabilities in creating content, automating processes, and enhancing decision-making. However, its rapid advancement has also opened the door to various monetization strategies that can sometimes be ethically questionable or even exploitative. Tech companies and startups are increasingly exploring ways to generate revenue from GenAI, often prioritizing profit over social responsibility.

One prevalent tactic is the subscription model, where users pay a recurring fee to access GenAI services. This model ensures a steady income stream and allows companies to continuously improve their algorithms. However, it can also create a digital divide, where only those who can afford the subscription can benefit from the technology. This raises ethical concerns about equal access to advanced tools and knowledge.

Another common strategy involves offering freemium services. Basic features are available for free, enticing users to engage with the platform, while advanced functionalities are locked behind a paywall. This approach can be particularly effective in attracting a large user base quickly. However, it often leads to the collection and monetization of user data. The free tier users become the product, as their data is analyzed, sold, or used to train the AI further, raising significant privacy issues.

Advertising is another lucrative monetization avenue. GenAI can generate highly personalized ads, increasing the likelihood of user engagement and, consequently, advertising revenue. While this can be seen as a win-win for businesses and advertisers, it also poses risks. The algorithms might prioritize content that maximizes ad engagement, which can sometimes mean promoting sensationalist or polarizing material. This tactic can contribute to misinformation and societal discord, all in the name of profit.

Licensing is also a common strategy, where companies develop GenAI solutions and license them to other businesses. This can be a highly profitable model, especially when the technology is niche or highly specialized. However, it can also lead to monopolistic practices, where a few companies control the majority of advanced GenAI tools, stifling competition and innovation.

Another monetization method involves the creation of proprietary datasets. Companies invest in collecting and curating large datasets, which are then used to train their GenAI models. These datasets can be sold or licensed to other firms, generating substantial revenue. The ethical dilemma here lies in the data collection process. Often, data is harvested without explicit consent, and individuals may be unaware that their personal information is being used for commercial gain.

Tokenization and blockchain integration offer yet another route for monetization. By creating digital tokens, companies can offer fractional ownership of their GenAI models or datasets. This method can democratize investment opportunities but also introduces volatility and speculation into the market. The focus shifts from technological advancement to financial gain, potentially compromising the quality and ethical standards of the AI solutions.

Crowdsourcing is another tactic where users contribute data, time, or computational power in exchange for access to GenAI services. While this can democratize access and foster community engagement, it often exploits users' contributions without fair compensation. The value generated from crowdsourced efforts disproportionately benefits the companies, not the individuals who contribute.

Each monetization tactic comes with its own set of ethical challenges. While GenAI offers immense potential for innovation and profit, the methods employed to monetize these technologies often prioritize financial gain over societal well-being. As such, it is crucial to scrutinize these tactics to ensure that the development and deployment of GenAI align with broader ethical standards and contribute positively to society.

Types of Scams

Generative Artificial Intelligence (GenAI) has revolutionized various sectors with its capabilities, but it has also opened the door to numerous types of scams. These scams leverage the advanced features of GenAI to deceive individuals and organizations. Understanding these scams is crucial for recognizing and mitigating their impact.

Phishing scams have evolved with the advent of GenAI. Traditional phishing involves sending fraudulent emails that appear to be from reputable sources to extract sensitive information. With GenAI, these emails have become more sophisticated. AI can generate personalized messages that mimic the writing style of trusted contacts, making them harder to detect. These messages often include links to fake websites designed to harvest login credentials or financial information.

Deepfake technology represents another significant threat. Deepfakes use GenAI to create hyper-realistic audio and video content that can impersonate individuals convincingly. Scammers use this technology to create fake videos of company executives or public figures, spreading misinformation or manipulating stock prices. Audio deepfakes can be used in vishing (voice phishing) attacks, where a scammer impersonates a trusted individual to extract confidential information over the phone.

Investment scams have also been enhanced by GenAI. Scammers use AI to analyze market trends and generate convincing investment opportunities. They create fake websites and social media profiles that appear legitimate, using AI-generated content to lure victims into investing in non-existent ventures. These scams often promise high returns with minimal risk, exploiting the victim's desire for quick financial gains.

Romance scams have seen a surge with GenAI's capabilities. Scammers create AI-generated profiles on dating sites and social media platforms, using attractive images and engaging conversation scripts to build trust and emotional connections with their targets. Once trust is established, they concoct stories of financial distress or urgent needs, persuading victims to transfer money. The emotional manipulation is so sophisticated that victims often fail to recognize the scam until it is too late.

Tech support scams have become more convincing with AI-generated chatbots. These scams typically start with a pop-up message or unsolicited call claiming that the victim's computer is infected with malware. The scammer then directs the victim to call a fake tech support number or download remote access software. AI chatbots can now handle these interactions, providing scripted responses that mimic genuine tech support, making the scam more believable.

Job scams have also been refined using GenAI. Scammers post fake job listings on legitimate job boards and social media platforms. They use AI to conduct interviews, generating responses that seem professional and legitimate. Once the victim is convinced of the job's authenticity, they are asked to pay for training materials, background checks, or other upfront costs. The scammer disappears once the payment is made, leaving the victim defrauded and jobless.

Lottery and sweepstakes scams have taken advantage of AI's ability to personalize messages. Victims receive messages claiming they have won a prize or lottery, often accompanied by official-looking documents generated by AI. The victim is then asked to pay taxes or fees to claim their winnings. The convincing nature of these messages, bolstered by AI, leads many to fall for the scam.

In the realm of cybersecurity, GenAI is used to automate and enhance attacks. AI can identify vulnerabilities in systems, craft targeted attacks, and adapt in real-time to security measures. This makes cyber attacks more efficient and harder to defend against, posing significant risks to individuals and organizations alike.

Understanding these scams is essential for developing strategies to protect against them. Awareness and education are the first lines of defense in recognizing and avoiding the sophisticated deceptions enabled by GenAI.

Economic Impact

The rise of Generative Artificial Intelligence (GenAI) has instigated profound economic shifts across various sectors. The technology's ability to create content, design products, and even simulate complex human tasks has expanded the horizons of productivity and innovation. However, these advancements come with significant economic implications that merit close examination.

One of the most notable impacts of GenAI is its influence on the labor market. Automation driven by GenAI threatens to displace a substantial number of jobs, particularly those involving routine and repetitive tasks. Industries such as manufacturing, customer service, and even creative fields like journalism and design are experiencing this shift. While automation can lead to increased efficiency and reduced operational costs, it also raises concerns about job security and the future of work. Workers in affected industries may need to adapt by acquiring new skills or transitioning to roles that require distinctly human capabilities, such as emotional intelligence and complex problem-solving.

On the flip side, GenAI has the potential to create new job opportunities and stimulate economic growth. The development, maintenance, and oversight of GenAI systems require specialized skills, leading to a surge in demand for AI experts, data scientists, and cybersecurity professionals. Moreover, sectors that leverage GenAI for innovation—such as pharmaceuticals, finance, and entertainment—could experience accelerated growth, resulting in new business models and revenue streams.

The economic benefits of GenAI extend beyond direct job creation. By enhancing productivity, GenAI can significantly boost economic output. For instance, in the healthcare sector, GenAI can streamline diagnostic processes, leading to faster and more accurate treatments. In agriculture, AI-driven predictive analytics can optimize crop yields and resource management. These improvements not only contribute to economic efficiency but also address critical global challenges such as healthcare accessibility and food security.

However, the economic gains from GenAI are not evenly distributed. There is a risk of exacerbating existing inequalities, both within and between countries. Developed nations with advanced technological infrastructures and substantial investment in AI research are better positioned to harness the benefits of GenAI. In contrast, developing countries may struggle to keep pace, potentially widening the economic divide. Within nations, the disparity between high-skilled workers who can adapt to AI-driven changes and low-skilled workers who are more vulnerable to job displacement could also increase.

Moreover, the economic landscape shaped by GenAI is not without regulatory and ethical challenges. The monopolization of GenAI technologies by a few dominant companies could stifle competition and innovation, leading to economic imbalances. Regulatory frameworks need to evolve to address issues such as data privacy, intellectual property rights, and the ethical use of AI. Governments and international bodies must work collaboratively to ensure that the economic benefits of GenAI are realized while mitigating potential risks.

Investment in education and training is crucial to prepare the workforce for the GenAI era. Policymakers, educational institutions, and industry leaders must prioritize initiatives that equip individuals with the skills needed to thrive in an AI-driven economy. Lifelong learning programs, vocational training, and public-private partnerships can play a pivotal role in this transition.

In summary, the economic impact of GenAI is multifaceted, offering both opportunities and challenges. While it promises significant productivity gains and new job creation, it also poses risks of job displacement and increased inequality. Navigating this complex landscape requires a balanced approach that embraces innovation while addressing the socio-economic implications of this transformative technology.

Detection and Prevention

Understanding and addressing the challenges posed by Generative Artificial Intelligence (GenAI) necessitates a robust framework for detection and prevention of its potential misuse. The rapid advancements in GenAI technology have made it increasingly difficult to distinguish between human-generated and AI-generated content, thereby complicating efforts to detect and mitigate the dark side of this powerful tool.

One of the primary methods for detecting AI-generated content involves the use of forensic analysis techniques. These techniques scrutinize the subtle inconsistencies and artifacts that often accompany AI-generated texts, images, or videos. For example, AI-generated images might exhibit unnatural textures, inconsistent lighting, or irregularities in fine details such as fingers or facial expressions. Similarly, AI-generated text can be identified through linguistic analysis, looking for patterns that are statistically unlikely in human writing, such as repetitive phrases or unusual syntax.

Another approach to detection is the deployment of machine learning models specifically trained to identify AI-generated content. These models analyze large datasets of both human and AI-generated material to learn distinctive features and patterns. Over time, they improve their accuracy in differentiating between the two. However, this method is a constant arms race, as GenAI systems also evolve and become more sophisticated, learning to mimic human behavior more convincingly.

Watermarking is a proactive prevention strategy that involves embedding a unique, invisible marker within AI-generated content. This marker can later be detected to verify the origin of the content, ensuring accountability and traceability. Watermarking is particularly useful for digital media, where it can help prevent unauthorized use and distribution of AI-generated works. However, the challenge lies in making these watermarks resilient to tampering while maintaining the quality of the content.

Another preventive measure is the implementation of stringent ethical guidelines and regulations governing the use of GenAI. Governments and institutions can establish frameworks that mandate transparency in AI-generated content, requiring creators to disclose when content is produced or augmented by AI. Such regulations could deter malicious actors by increasing the legal and social repercussions of misuse. Moreover, fostering a culture of ethical AI development within the tech community is essential. Encouraging developers to adhere to principles of fairness, accountability, and transparency can mitigate the risks associated with GenAI.

Education and public awareness also play a crucial role in prevention. By informing the public about the capabilities and limitations of GenAI, individuals can become more discerning consumers of digital content. Media literacy programs that teach critical thinking and analytical skills can empower people to question the authenticity of what they see and read, reducing the impact of misinformation and deepfakes.

Collaborative efforts between the tech industry, academia, and governments are vital for staying ahead of the curve. Joint initiatives can lead to the development of advanced detection tools and the establishment of best practices for AI governance. Sharing knowledge and resources can enhance the collective ability to combat the misuse of GenAI.

Investing in research and development of AI technologies that prioritize safety and ethical considerations is another key aspect. By focusing on creating AI systems that are inherently secure and transparent, developers can preemptively address potential threats. This includes designing AI with built-in safeguards that limit its ability to generate harmful or deceptive content.

Balancing the benefits of GenAI with the need to prevent its dark side requires a multifaceted approach. Through a combination of advanced detection techniques, proactive prevention strategies, regulatory frameworks, public education, and collaborative efforts, society can harness the power of GenAI while mitigating its potential risks.

Policy Recommendations

Addressing the complexities of generative artificial intelligence (GenAI) requires a multifaceted approach that incorporates ethical, legal, and technological considerations. Policymakers must develop robust frameworks to mitigate potential risks while fostering innovation. One of the first steps is to establish comprehensive regulatory guidelines that clearly define the boundaries of acceptable use for GenAI technologies. These guidelines should emphasize transparency, accountability, and the protection of individual rights.

To enhance transparency, it is crucial to mandate that developers disclose the data sources and algorithms used in GenAI systems. This ensures that users and regulators can scrutinize the origins and biases embedded within these technologies. Additionally, implementing standardized auditing processes can help verify the integrity and fairness of GenAI models.

Regular audits conducted by independent bodies would facilitate trust and compliance with ethical standards.

Accountability can be reinforced by creating a legal framework that holds developers and organizations responsible for the outcomes of their GenAI systems. This includes establishing liability for harms caused by AI-generated content, such as misinformation, defamation, or privacy breaches. Clear legal recourse should be available for individuals adversely affected by these technologies, ensuring that victims have a path to seek redress.

Protection of individual rights is another critical area that requires attention. Privacy regulations should be updated to address the unique challenges posed by GenAI. This includes safeguarding personal data from unauthorized use and preventing the creation of synthetic identities that can be exploited for malicious purposes. Policies should also ensure that AI-generated content does not infringe on intellectual property rights, protecting creators and innovators.

In addition to regulatory measures, fostering collaboration between governments, academia, and industry is essential. Establishing interdisciplinary research initiatives can help identify emerging risks and develop best practices for GenAI deployment. Public-private partnerships can facilitate the sharing of knowledge and resources, accelerating the development of safe and ethical AI technologies.

Education and awareness programs are vital to equip the public and stakeholders with the knowledge needed to navigate the GenAI landscape. By promoting digital literacy and ethical AI practices, society can better understand the implications of these technologies and make informed decisions. Training programs for developers and engineers should emphasize ethical considerations and the social impact of their work, fostering a culture of responsibility within the tech industry.

International cooperation is also crucial in addressing the global nature of GenAI. Harmonizing regulations and standards across borders can prevent regulatory arbitrage and ensure a consistent approach to AI governance. Collaborative efforts through international organizations can facilitate the exchange of best practices and promote the development of global norms for GenAI.

Investment in research and development for AI safety and ethics is necessary to stay ahead of the rapidly evolving GenAI landscape. Funding for interdisciplinary studies that explore the ethical, social, and technical aspects of AI can provide valuable insights and inform policy decisions. Encouraging innovation in AI safety mechanisms, such as explainable AI and robust adversarial defenses, can enhance the reliability and security of GenAI systems.

By implementing these policy recommendations, society can harness the benefits of GenAI while minimizing its dark side. Comprehensive regulations, accountability measures, collaborative efforts, and continuous research are essential components of a balanced approach to managing the complexities of generative artificial intelligence.

11. Harassment and Maximizing Reach

Forms of Harassment

Generative Artificial Intelligence (GenAI) has revolutionized various facets of modern life, from automating mundane tasks to creating sophisticated art. However, alongside its numerous benefits, it has also introduced new avenues for harassment. These manifestations of digital abuse are diverse, often sophisticated, and can have severe consequences for individuals and communities. Understanding the various forms of harassment enabled by GenAI is crucial for developing effective countermeasures.

One prominent form of harassment facilitated by GenAI is deepfake technology. Deepfakes use advanced algorithms to create hyper-realistic videos and audio recordings that depict individuals saying or doing things they never did. This technology has been weaponized to create non-consensual pornography, manipulate public opinion, and tarnish reputations. The victims of deepfake harassment often find themselves in a state of helplessness, as proving the inauthenticity of these fabricated materials can be exceedingly challenging.

Another significant form of harassment is automated trolling. GenAI can generate endless streams of abusive messages, tweets, or comments, overwhelming the target and making digital spaces hostile. These automated trolls can mimic human behavior convincingly, making it difficult to filter out harassment using traditional moderation techniques. This form of harassment can lead to severe emotional distress, driving individuals away from online platforms and silencing their voices.

Impersonation is also a critical issue exacerbated by GenAI. Advanced AI can create realistic social media profiles, complete with fabricated backstories and interactions. These fake personas can be used to deceive, manipulate, or harass individuals. For example, a harasser might create a profile that mimics a victim's friend or family member, using it to gain their trust and then betray or exploit them. This kind of harassment can erode trust in online interactions and cause significant psychological harm.

AI-driven stalking is another alarming form of harassment. GenAI can analyze vast amounts of data to track and predict an individual's movements, preferences, and activities. This information can then be used to create detailed profiles that stalkers can exploit to monitor and harass their targets. The pervasive nature of AI-driven stalking makes it incredibly invasive, stripping individuals of their privacy and sense of security.

Moreover, GenAI can be utilized to amplify doxxing attacks, where private information about an individual is publicly disclosed without their consent. AI can scour the internet for personal data, compile it, and disseminate it quickly and efficiently. This form of harassment can lead to real-world consequences, such as threats, job loss, and emotional trauma, as victims find their private lives exposed to the public.

Finally, AI-generated misinformation and defamation represent another insidious form of harassment. GenAI can produce convincing but false narratives that spread rapidly across social media and other platforms. These falsehoods can damage reputations, incite harassment from others, and create a toxic environment for the victim. The speed and scale at which AI can generate and distribute such content make it a formidable tool for harassers.

Understanding these various forms of harassment is essential for developing strategies to mitigate their impact. As GenAI continues to evolve, so too must our approaches to safeguarding individuals from its darker applications. By recognizing the potential for abuse, society can better prepare to address and combat the challenges posed by this powerful technology.

Techniques for Maximizing Reach

In the rapidly evolving landscape of Generative AI (GenAI), maximizing reach is a critical aspect that dictates the effectiveness and influence of AI-generated content. Various techniques can be employed to ensure that the content not only reaches a vast audience but also resonates with them on multiple levels. Understanding these techniques is essential for anyone looking to harness the full potential of GenAI.

One of the foremost techniques involves leveraging social media platforms. These platforms have become the epicenters of digital communication, and their algorithms are designed to amplify content that garners engagement. By strategically timing posts, using relevant hashtags, and creating shareable content, one can significantly boost the visibility of AI-generated material. Additionally, understanding the nuances of each platform—whether it be the brevity required for Twitter, the visual appeal necessary for Instagram, or the professional tone suited for LinkedIn—can further enhance reach.

Another effective technique is Search Engine Optimization (SEO). SEO involves tailoring content to align with the algorithms that search engines use to rank websites. By incorporating relevant keywords, optimizing meta descriptions, and ensuring high-quality backlinks, AI-generated content can achieve higher rankings on search engine results pages. This not only increases visibility but also drives organic traffic to the content, thereby expanding its reach.

Collaborations and partnerships also play a pivotal role in maximizing reach. By collaborating with influencers, experts, or other entities within a specific niche, AI-generated content can tap into established audiences. These collaborations can take various forms, including guest posts, joint webinars, or co-branded content. The credibility and reach of the partners can lend additional weight to the AI-generated material, making it more appealing and trustworthy to a broader audience.

Personalization is another powerful technique. AI has the capability to analyze vast amounts of data to create highly personalized content that caters to individual preferences and behaviors. By delivering tailored experiences, the content is more likely to engage users and encourage them to share it within their networks. This personalized approach not only maximizes reach but also fosters a deeper connection with the audience.

Utilizing multimedia elements is equally important. The integration of images, videos, infographics, and interactive elements can make AI-generated content more engaging and shareable. Multimedia content is often more appealing and can convey complex information more effectively than text alone. This can lead to higher engagement rates and, consequently, a wider reach.

Content distribution strategies also need to be meticulously planned and executed. This includes using email marketing campaigns, syndicating content across various platforms, and employing paid advertising. Each of these channels has its own set of best practices and can be optimized to ensure maximum reach. For instance, segmenting email lists to target specific demographics can result in higher open and click-through rates, while paid advertising can be fine-tuned to reach a highly targeted audience.

Lastly, continuous monitoring and analysis are crucial for refining these techniques. By using analytics tools to track performance metrics such as engagement rates, click-through rates, and conversion rates, one can gain insights into what works and what doesn't. This data-driven approach allows for ongoing adjustments and improvements, ensuring that the strategies remain effective over time.

Incorporating these techniques requires a multifaceted approach, combining strategic planning, data analysis, and creative execution. By doing so, the reach of AI-generated content can be maximized, ensuring that it not only reaches a broad audience but also makes a meaningful impact.

Impact on Victims

The proliferation of Generative Artificial Intelligence (GenAI) has brought about significant advancements in various fields, from creative arts to scientific research. However, beneath the surface of these innovations lies a darker reality, particularly for those who find themselves as unwitting victims of its misuse. The impact on victims of GenAI can be profound, affecting their personal, professional, and psychological well-being in multiple ways.

One of the most immediate and tangible effects on victims is the loss of privacy. GenAI can generate realistic images, videos, and audio clips, often indistinguishable from real ones. This capability has been exploited to create deepfakes—manipulated media that can depict individuals in compromising or misleading situations. Victims of deepfakes may find their reputations tarnished, relationships strained, and careers jeopardized. The psychological toll of knowing that one's likeness can be so easily manipulated and disseminated without consent is considerable, leading to feelings of vulnerability and anxiety.

Another significant impact is the spread of misinformation and its consequences. GenAI can be used to create and propagate false information at an unprecedented scale and speed. This can lead to public defamation, where individuals are falsely portrayed in negative lights, affecting their social standing and mental health. For public figures, this can mean a loss of credibility and public trust; for private citizens, it can result in severe social ostracization and emotional distress.

Economic harm is another critical aspect. Victims of GenAI-generated fraud and identity theft can suffer substantial financial losses. GenAI tools can generate convincing fake identities or clone existing ones, facilitating various forms of cybercrime. Victims may find their bank accounts drained, credit scores damaged, and personal information sold on the dark web. The process of recovering from such an attack is often lengthy and stressful, involving legal battles, financial reparations, and a constant fear of recurrence.

The psychological impact on victims cannot be understated. The sense of helplessness and invasion of personal space can lead to severe mental health issues, including depression, anxiety, and post-traumatic stress disorder (PTSD). The knowledge that one's identity or personal information can be manipulated and misused by GenAI creates a pervasive sense of insecurity. Victims often struggle with trust issues, fearing that anyone they interact with could be using or sharing their information maliciously.

Furthermore, the social implications can be devastating. Victims may face stigmatization and alienation from their communities. The social fallout from being associated with false or damaging content can lead to isolation and a breakdown of support systems. This isolation exacerbates the psychological distress, creating a vicious cycle that is difficult to break.

Legal recourse for victims is often limited and inadequate. The rapid evolution of GenAI technologies outpaces the development of regulatory frameworks, leaving victims with few avenues for redress. Existing laws may not cover the specific nuances of GenAI-related offenses, and the global nature of the internet complicates jurisdictional issues. This legal grey area adds to the frustration and helplessness experienced by victims.

In essence, while GenAI holds the promise of transformative benefits, its potential for harm is equally significant. The impact on victims is multifaceted, encompassing privacy violations, misinformation, economic loss, psychological trauma, social stigmatization, and inadequate legal protection. Addressing these issues requires a comprehensive approach, involving technological safeguards, legal reforms, and societal awareness to mitigate the dark side of GenAI.

Legal Measures

Legal frameworks and regulations have become increasingly critical in addressing the multifaceted challenges posed by the rise of Generative AI (GenAI). As these advanced systems continue to evolve, their pervasive influence on various sectors necessitates a robust legal response to mitigate potential risks and ethical dilemmas.

One of the primary concerns that legal measures aim to address is the issue of intellectual property (IP). GenAI systems, which can generate content ranging from text and music to visual art, often do so by training on vast datasets that may include copyrighted material. This raises significant questions about the ownership and rights associated with the AI-generated outputs. Existing IP laws are frequently ill-equipped to handle these complexities. Consequently, there is a growing call for redefining IP regulations to ensure that creators of original works are adequately protected and compensated, even as GenAI systems leverage their creations.

Privacy is another critical area where legal measures are essential. GenAI systems often require extensive datasets, which can include sensitive personal information. The collection, storage, and use of such data must comply with stringent privacy regulations to prevent misuse and protect individuals' rights. Laws such as the General Data Protection Regulation (GDPR) in Europe set a precedent by imposing strict guidelines on data handling practices. However, the rapid advancement of GenAI technologies necessitates continuous updates to these regulations to address emerging privacy challenges effectively.

Bias and discrimination present further legal and ethical concerns. GenAI systems can inadvertently perpetuate and even amplify existing biases present in the training data. This can lead to discriminatory outcomes in applications such as hiring processes, loan approvals, and law enforcement. Legal measures must, therefore, include provisions for auditing and mitigating biases in AI systems. Ensuring transparency and accountability in the development and deployment of GenAI is crucial. Regulations that mandate regular bias assessments and the implementation of corrective measures can help in creating fairer and more equitable AI systems.

The potential misuse of GenAI for malicious purposes, such as generating deepfakes or facilitating cyber-attacks, underscores the need for stringent legal measures. Governments and regulatory bodies must establish clear guidelines and penalties for the misuse of GenAI technologies. This includes not only criminalizing the creation and distribution of harmful content but also holding developers and users accountable for the ethical implications of their AI systems. International cooperation is vital in this regard, as the global nature of GenAI technologies requires a unified approach to regulation and enforcement.

Moreover, the rapid pace of GenAI development poses challenges for existing regulatory frameworks, which can often lag behind technological advancements. To address this, legal measures must be adaptive and forward-looking. Regulatory sandboxes, where new technologies can be tested in a controlled environment under the supervision of regulators, offer a promising approach. These sandboxes allow for real-time assessment and adjustment of regulations, ensuring that they remain relevant and effective in the face of evolving GenAI technologies.

Ethical considerations are integral to the legal discourse surrounding GenAI. Establishing ethical guidelines and standards for the development and use of GenAI can help in navigating the moral complexities associated with these technologies. Legal measures should incorporate ethical principles, ensuring that AI systems are designed and deployed in ways that align with societal values and public interest.

In summary, the legal landscape for GenAI is intricate and continually evolving. Addressing the challenges posed by these advanced systems requires a comprehensive and dynamic approach to regulation. By focusing on intellectual property, privacy, bias, misuse, adaptability, and ethics, legal measures can play a crucial role in harnessing the benefits of GenAI while mitigating its potential harms.

Support Mechanisms

While the transformative potential of General Artificial Intelligence (GenAI) is often lauded, it is essential to recognize the robust support mechanisms that underpin its operation. These mechanisms ensure that GenAI systems function effectively, ethically, and safely. They encompass a variety of frameworks, including technical infrastructure, regulatory guidelines, and ethical oversight, each playing a critical role in the broader GenAI ecosystem.

At the technical level, the infrastructure supporting GenAI is both intricate and expansive. High-performance computing resources, such as powerful GPUs and distributed cloud networks, are foundational. These elements facilitate the immense computational demands required for training and deploying GenAI models. Data storage solutions, capable of handling vast amounts of information, are also crucial. They ensure that data is not only stored securely but is also readily accessible for real-time processing and analysis. Moreover, robust cybersecurity measures are implemented to protect against data breaches and cyber-attacks, which could compromise the integrity and confidentiality of the data used by GenAI systems.

Regulatory frameworks form another cornerstone of the support mechanisms for GenAI. Governments and international bodies have begun to establish comprehensive guidelines to govern the development and deployment of GenAI technologies. These regulations aim to safeguard public interest by ensuring that GenAI operates within the bounds of the law and ethical standards. They address various issues, from data privacy to accountability in decision-making processes. For instance, the General Data Protection Regulation (GDPR) in the European Union has set a precedent for stringent data protection standards that GenAI systems must adhere to. Compliance with such regulations is not merely a legal obligation but also a critical component in building public trust in GenAI technologies.

Ethical oversight is equally vital in the realm of GenAI. Ethical committees and boards are often established within organizations to oversee the deployment and use of GenAI. These bodies are tasked with identifying potential ethical dilemmas and ensuring that the technology is used responsibly. They evaluate the societal impacts of GenAI, considering factors such as bias, fairness, and transparency. By conducting thorough ethical reviews, these committees help to prevent discriminatory practices and promote equitable outcomes. Additionally, they advocate for the inclusion of diverse perspectives in the development process, ensuring that GenAI systems are designed with a broad range of human experiences in mind.

Education and training programs also serve as essential support mechanisms for GenAI. These initiatives aim to equip individuals with the necessary skills and knowledge to work with GenAI technologies effectively. Universities and research institutions offer specialized courses and degrees focused on artificial intelligence and machine learning. Continuous professional development programs are also available for those already in the field, ensuring that practitioners stay abreast of the latest advancements and best practices. By fostering a well-informed and skilled workforce, these educational efforts contribute to the responsible and innovative deployment of GenAI.

In addition to these formal mechanisms, community-driven efforts play a significant role in supporting GenAI. Open-source platforms and collaborative projects enable researchers and developers to share knowledge, resources, and tools. These collaborative environments foster innovation and facilitate the rapid advancement of GenAI technologies. They also promote transparency and accountability, as the open nature of these projects allows for peer review and scrutiny.

Together, these support mechanisms form a comprehensive framework that sustains the development and deployment of GenAI. They ensure that the technology not only achieves its full potential but does so in a manner that is ethical, secure, and beneficial to society.

12. Fake Digital Personas and Falsified Media

Creating Fake Personas

Generative Artificial Intelligence (GenAI) has made significant strides, enabling the creation of highly sophisticated and realistic digital personas. These personas, often indistinguishable from real individuals, can be generated with alarming ease. This capability poses significant ethical and security challenges, as it opens the door to a variety of malicious activities.

At the core of creating fake personas is the ability of GenAI to synthesize human-like features and behaviors. The technology leverages vast amounts of data to generate images, voices, and even personality traits that mimic real people. Advanced algorithms analyze facial structures, vocal patterns, and social behaviors to create digital entities that can seamlessly integrate into online environments. These personas can be tailored to meet specific objectives, whether for marketing purposes, social engineering, or more nefarious activities like identity theft and espionage.

One of the primary tools used in the creation of these personas is the Generative Adversarial Network (GAN). GANs consist of two neural networks—the generator and the discriminator—that work in tandem to produce highly realistic outputs. The generator creates images or data points, while the discriminator evaluates their authenticity. Through continuous iterations, the generator improves its output, resulting in highly convincing digital personas. These personas can be further refined by incorporating additional layers of data, such as social media activity, communication styles, and even psychological profiles.

The implications of creating fake personas extend beyond the digital realm. For instance, in the political arena, fake personas can be used to manipulate public opinion, spread misinformation, and even interfere with electoral processes. By creating seemingly credible sources, malicious actors can sway public discourse and undermine democratic institutions. Similarly, in the corporate world, fake personas can be used for industrial espionage, gaining access to sensitive information under false pretenses.

Moreover, the rise of social media platforms has provided fertile ground for the proliferation of fake personas. These platforms often lack robust verification mechanisms, making it easier for malicious actors to create and deploy digital entities. Once established, these personas can interact with real users, build networks, and even influence social trends. The anonymity and reach afforded by social media further exacerbate the problem, making it difficult to trace and eliminate fake personas.

The commercial sector is not immune to the risks posed by fake personas. Companies can use them for deceptive marketing practices, creating fake reviews and endorsements to manipulate consumer behavior. This not only undermines consumer trust but also distorts market dynamics. Regulatory bodies are increasingly aware of these risks, but the rapid pace of technological advancement often outstrips the development of effective countermeasures.

Addressing the challenges posed by fake personas requires a multi-faceted approach. Technological solutions, such as improved verification mechanisms and AI-driven detection tools, are essential. However, these must be complemented by robust regulatory frameworks and public awareness campaigns. Educating users about the potential risks and encouraging critical evaluation of online information can help mitigate the impact of fake personas.

In essence, the creation of fake personas through GenAI represents a double-edged sword. While the technology offers unprecedented opportunities for innovation, it also poses significant ethical and security challenges. As GenAI continues to evolve, it is imperative to address these challenges proactively, ensuring that the technology is used responsibly and ethically.

Falsified Media Types

Generative AI (GenAI) has revolutionized the creation and manipulation of digital content, but it has also opened the door to numerous ethical and societal concerns. One of the most pressing issues is the proliferation of falsified media types. These are not merely limited to deepfakes, which have garnered significant public attention; they encompass a range of manipulated content that can deceive, mislead, and manipulate audiences.

Deepfakes, created using sophisticated machine learning algorithms, enable the production of hyper-realistic videos and audio recordings that are almost indistinguishable from genuine footage. This technology can superimpose one person's face onto another's body or synthesize a person's voice to say things they never actually said. While deepfakes can be used for entertainment and creative purposes, they also pose severe risks when used maliciously. For instance, deepfakes can be employed to fabricate evidence, spread misinformation, or damage reputations, leading to significant consequences for individuals and society.

Another form of falsified media generated by GenAI is synthetic text. Language models, such as GPT-3, can produce coherent and contextually relevant text that mimics human writing. This capability can be exploited to create fake news articles, misleading social media posts, or fraudulent academic papers. The ease with which these texts can be generated makes it challenging to discern authentic content from fabricated material, thereby exacerbating the spread of misinformation and eroding public trust in information sources.

AI-generated images are another area where falsified media types are prevalent. These images can range from entirely fictitious portraits of non-existent people to altered photographs that change the context or content of the original image. Tools like GANs (Generative Adversarial Networks) have made it possible to create highly realistic images that can be used in various deceptive ways. For example, fake images can be used in advertising to promote products that do not exist or in political campaigns to smear opponents.

Audio deepfakes, or "voice cloning," are equally concerning. Advances in AI have made it possible to replicate a person's voice with high accuracy, enabling the creation of audio recordings where someone appears to say things they never did. This technology can be used for malicious purposes, such as creating fake audio evidence for legal cases, conducting fraudulent phone scams, or impersonating individuals in sensitive communications.

The implications of these falsified media types are far-reaching. They can undermine the credibility of legitimate media, making it increasingly difficult for the public to distinguish between real and fake content. This erosion of trust can lead to a more polarized and skeptical society, where misinformation flourishes, and the veracity of information is constantly questioned.

To combat the spread of falsified media, it is essential to develop and implement robust detection technologies. Researchers and tech companies are working on algorithms that can identify deepfakes and other manipulated content, but these solutions are constantly in a race against the ever-evolving capabilities of GenAI. Additionally, there is a need for greater public awareness and media literacy to help individuals critically evaluate the information they encounter.

Legislation and regulations may also play a role in addressing the challenges posed by falsified media. Governments and international bodies have begun to recognize the threat and are exploring ways to regulate the use and dissemination of such content. However, balancing the regulation of AI-generated media with the protection of freedom of expression remains a complex and delicate issue.

In essence, while GenAI offers remarkable opportunities, it also necessitates vigilance and proactive measures to mitigate the risks associated with falsified media types.

Detection Techniques

The rapid proliferation of generative artificial intelligence (GenAI) has brought forth a plethora of applications, from creative content generation to advanced problem-solving. However, this technological marvel also harbors a darker side, where its capabilities can be misused for malicious activities such as deepfakes, misinformation, and cyberattacks. Detecting these malevolent uses of GenAI is critical to mitigating their impact and safeguarding society. Several sophisticated detection techniques have been developed to address this challenge.

One of the primary methods involves the use of machine learning algorithms to identify anomalies indicative of GenAI-generated content. These algorithms are trained on vast datasets containing both genuine and artificially generated data. By analyzing patterns and discrepancies, such as inconsistencies in pixel arrangements in images or unnatural language patterns in text, these systems can flag potential GenAI outputs. For instance, convolutional neural networks (CNNs) have shown promise in detecting deepfakes by scrutinizing subtle details that are often overlooked by the human eye.

Another approach leverages the concept of digital forensics. This technique entails examining the metadata and provenance of digital content. Metadata, which includes information about the creation, modification, and transmission of a file, can reveal telltale signs of manipulation. For example, discrepancies in the timestamps or the absence of a clear source can raise red flags. In the case of images and videos, forensic experts may also analyze the compression artifacts and noise patterns that differ between authentic and synthesized media.

Watermarking is an additional strategy employed to combat the misuse of GenAI. This involves embedding invisible markers within digital content that can be used to verify its authenticity. These markers, often imperceptible to human senses, can be detected using specialized software. Watermarking not only aids in identifying GenAI-generated material but also serves as a deterrent against unauthorized use. By ensuring that content creators can trace their work, this technique helps maintain the integrity of digital media.

Natural Language Processing (NLP) techniques are particularly useful in detecting AI-generated text. NLP algorithms can analyze the syntax, semantics, and context of written content to identify irregularities. For example, AI-generated text may exhibit unnatural phrasing, repetitive structures, or contextually inappropriate word choices. Advanced NLP models can compare the suspect text against a corpus of human-written documents to assess its authenticity. Additionally, linguistic forensics can be employed to examine stylistic elements such as writing tone, vocabulary richness, and sentence complexity.

Blockchain technology offers a novel solution to the problem of verifying digital content. By creating a decentralized and immutable ledger of digital transactions, blockchain ensures that any alterations to the content are recorded and traceable. This transparency enables the verification of the authenticity and history of digital assets, making it significantly harder for malicious actors to propagate GenAI-generated material without detection.

Collaboration between technology developers, regulatory bodies, and cybersecurity experts is essential to enhancing these detection techniques. Continuous advancements in AI and machine learning require adaptive and evolving strategies to stay ahead of malicious uses. Public awareness and education also play a crucial role in combating the dark side of GenAI. By understanding the potential risks and the available detection methods, individuals and organizations can better protect themselves against the threats posed by this powerful technology.

In an era where the lines between reality and artificiality are increasingly blurred, robust detection techniques are indispensable. They form the first line of defense in preserving the integrity of digital content and ensuring that the benefits of GenAI are not overshadowed by its potential for misuse.

Case Studies

The rapid advancement and integration of Generative Artificial Intelligence (GenAI) have brought about remarkable transformations across various industries. However, the potential for misuse and unintended consequences has also surfaced, highlighting the darker aspects of this technology. Examining specific instances where GenAI has been employed can provide valuable insights into its complex nature.

A notable case involves the use of GenAI in the creation and dissemination of deepfake videos. Deepfakes leverage GenAI to fabricate highly realistic videos by superimposing the likeness of individuals onto other bodies or altering their speech and actions. In one high-profile instance, a deepfake video featuring a prominent political figure went viral, spreading misinformation and causing public outrage. The video was so convincing that it took experts considerable effort to debunk it. This incident underscores the potential for GenAI to erode trust in digital media and manipulate public opinion.

Another significant example is the application of GenAI in automated content generation. Several companies have adopted GenAI to produce articles, social media posts, and even creative writing. While this has increased efficiency and content volume, it has also led to ethical dilemmas. In one case, a news organization used GenAI to write articles on sensitive topics, resulting in content that lacked the nuanced understanding and empathy of human writers. The articles, though factually accurate, were criticized for their insensitivity and failure to capture the human element of the stories. This highlights the limitations of GenAI in contexts that require deep emotional intelligence and ethical consideration.

In the realm of cybersecurity, GenAI has been a double-edged sword. On one hand, it has been instrumental in developing sophisticated tools for threat detection and response. On the other hand, malicious actors have exploited GenAI to enhance cyber-attacks. A particularly troubling case involved the use of GenAI to craft highly personalized phishing emails. These emails were so well-tailored to the recipients that they bypassed traditional security filters and led to significant data breaches. This incident illustrates the arms race between cybersecurity measures and the increasingly sophisticated methods employed by cybercriminals, fueled by GenAI.

The use of GenAI in healthcare also presents a complex picture. On one side, GenAI has contributed to advancements in medical research, diagnostics, and patient care. However, there have been instances where its application has raised ethical concerns. For example, a healthcare provider used GenAI to predict patient outcomes and prioritize treatment. While the technology improved efficiency, it also inadvertently introduced biases based on the data it was trained on. Patients from underrepresented groups received lower priority, highlighting the risk of perpetuating existing inequalities through biased algorithms.

In education, GenAI has been employed to develop personalized learning experiences, offering tailored content and assessments for students. However, a case involving the use of GenAI in grading revealed significant flaws. An algorithm designed to grade student essays was found to disproportionately favor certain writing styles and penalize others, leading to unfair evaluations. This case emphasizes the need for transparency and oversight in the deployment of GenAI in educational settings to ensure fairness and equity.

These examples illustrate the multifaceted impact of GenAI across different sectors. While the technology holds immense potential, its application must be carefully managed to mitigate risks and address ethical concerns. The dark side of GenAI is not inherent to the technology itself but arises from its misuse and the lack of adequate safeguards. As society continues to navigate the complexities of GenAI, it is crucial to strike a balance between innovation and responsibility.

Preventative Measures

The rapid advancement of Generative AI (GenAI) has brought forth a myriad of challenges and ethical concerns that must be addressed to prevent misuse and potential harm. Implementing preventative measures is crucial to ensure that GenAI technologies are developed and employed responsibly. Several strategies can be adopted to mitigate risks and promote a framework that prioritizes safety, transparency, and ethical considerations.

First and foremost, robust regulatory frameworks are essential. Governments and international bodies need to collaborate to establish comprehensive guidelines that govern the development and deployment of GenAI. These regulations should encompass aspects such as data privacy, algorithmic accountability, and ethical use. By setting clear standards and enforcing compliance, it is possible to create an environment where GenAI can thrive without compromising societal values.

Another vital preventative measure is the adoption of ethical AI design principles. Developers and researchers should be encouraged to integrate ethical considerations into the design and implementation of GenAI systems from the outset. This includes ensuring fairness, avoiding bias, and maintaining transparency in decision-making processes. By embedding these principles into the core of AI development, the risk of harmful outcomes can be significantly reduced.

Education and awareness play a critical role in preventing the misuse of GenAI. It is imperative to educate both the public and professionals about the potential risks and ethical implications associated with GenAI. This can be achieved through public awareness campaigns, training programs, and academic courses that focus on AI ethics and responsible usage. An informed and vigilant society is better equipped to identify and counteract the malicious use of GenAI technologies.

Investing in research dedicated to AI safety is another crucial step. By allocating resources to study the potential dangers and vulnerabilities of

GenAI, researchers can develop advanced techniques to detect and mitigate risks. This includes creating more robust algorithms that can resist adversarial attacks, developing methods to ensure data integrity, and enhancing the interpretability of AI models. Proactive research efforts can help anticipate and address issues before they escalate.

Collaboration between stakeholders is also essential. The development and deployment of GenAI involve multiple parties, including tech companies, researchers, policymakers, and end-users. Fostering a collaborative environment where these stakeholders can share knowledge, best practices, and resources is vital. Such cooperation can lead to the creation of industry-wide standards and the establishment of a collective approach to tackling the challenges posed by GenAI.

Transparency in AI systems is a critical preventative measure. Developers should strive to make AI models more interpretable and explainable, allowing users to understand how decisions are made. This can build trust and enable users to identify and report any anomalies or biases in AI behavior. Transparency also facilitates accountability, as it becomes easier to trace the origins of errors or unethical practices.

Finally, the implementation of robust monitoring and auditing mechanisms is necessary. Continuous monitoring of GenAI systems can help detect and rectify any deviations from ethical standards or regulatory requirements. Regular audits by independent bodies can ensure that AI systems operate within the established guidelines and maintain their intended purpose without causing harm.

By adopting these preventative measures, it is possible to harness the potential of GenAI while minimizing the associated risks. A proactive and comprehensive approach to regulation, ethical design, education, research, collaboration, transparency, and monitoring can pave the way for a future where GenAI contributes positively to society.

13. Ethical and Safety Implications

Ethical Considerations

Generative Artificial Intelligence (GenAI) has rapidly evolved, presenting unprecedented opportunities and challenges. As this technology advances, ethical considerations become paramount. The potential for misuse and unintended consequences necessitates a thorough examination of the moral landscape surrounding GenAI.

One significant ethical issue is the potential for bias and discrimination in GenAI systems. These systems often rely on vast datasets to train their algorithms. If the data used is biased, the AI can perpetuate and even amplify these biases. For instance, if a GenAI system is trained on data that underrepresents certain demographics, it may produce outputs that unfairly discriminate against those groups. This can have serious repercussions in areas such as hiring practices, law enforcement, and healthcare, where biased decisions can lead to unequal treatment and exacerbate existing social inequalities.

Privacy concerns also arise with the use of GenAI. These systems often require large amounts of personal data to function effectively. The collection, storage, and use of this data pose significant risks to individual privacy. There is the potential for data breaches, unauthorized access, and misuse of sensitive information. Additionally, the ability of GenAI to generate realistic synthetic data, such as deepfakes, raises concerns about consent and the potential for malicious use. Ensuring that data is handled ethically and that individuals' privacy is protected is crucial.

The transparency and accountability of GenAI systems are also critical ethical considerations. Many GenAI models operate as "black boxes," meaning their decision-making processes are not easily understood. This lack of transparency can make it difficult to hold these systems accountable for their actions. If a GenAI system makes a harmful or unfair decision, it is challenging to determine the cause and rectify the issue. Developing methods to improve the interpretability and transparency of these systems is essential to ensure they can be held accountable for their outputs.

The potential for job displacement is another ethical concern associated with GenAI. As these systems become more capable, they may replace human workers in various industries. While this technological advancement can lead to increased efficiency and productivity, it also raises questions about the socioeconomic impact on displaced workers. Addressing this concern involves considering how to support workers transitioning to new roles and ensuring that the benefits of GenAI are distributed equitably across society.

Moreover, the dual-use nature of GenAI technology poses significant ethical challenges. While GenAI can be used for beneficial purposes, such as improving medical diagnoses or creating educational content, it can also be exploited for malicious purposes. This includes generating fake news, creating misleading information, or even developing autonomous weapons. The dual-use dilemma necessitates careful consideration of how to regulate and control the use of GenAI to prevent its misuse while promoting its positive applications.

Ethical considerations in GenAI are multifaceted and complex. Addressing these issues requires a collaborative effort involving technologists, ethicists, policymakers, and society at large. Developing robust ethical frameworks, implementing regulatory measures, and fostering an ongoing dialogue about the implications of GenAI are crucial steps in navigating the ethical landscape of this powerful technology. By doing so, it is possible to harness the benefits of GenAI while mitigating its risks and ensuring it is used responsibly and ethically.

Safety Concerns

Generative AI (GenAI) has undoubtedly revolutionized numerous fields, from natural language processing to image generation. However, alongside its promising capabilities, significant safety concerns arise that necessitate careful examination. One of the most pressing issues is the potential for misuse. GenAI can be weaponized to create deepfakes, highly realistic but fake audiovisual content. These deepfakes can be used for malicious purposes such as blackmail, spreading misinformation, or manipulating public opinion. The technology's ability to fabricate convincing yet false narratives poses a threat to societal trust and stability.

Another safety concern revolves around the inherent biases present in GenAI systems. These biases often stem from the training data, which may reflect historical and societal prejudices. When these biases are ingrained in GenAI models, they can perpetuate and even exacerbate discrimination in various applications, such as hiring processes, law enforcement, and content moderation. Addressing these biases is crucial to prevent the reinforcement of harmful stereotypes and ensure equitable outcomes.

The opacity of GenAI models also contributes to safety concerns. Many GenAI systems operate as "black boxes," meaning their decision-making processes are not transparent. This lack of transparency makes it challenging to understand why a model made a particular decision or to identify potential errors. In critical applications, such as medical diagnosis or autonomous driving, this opacity can lead to catastrophic consequences if the system makes an incorrect decision. Developing methods for explainability and transparency in GenAI is essential to mitigate these risks.

Additionally, the rapid advancement of GenAI technology raises concerns about the pace of regulation and oversight. Policymakers and regulatory bodies often struggle to keep up with the fast-evolving landscape of AI technologies. Without adequate regulation, there is a risk that GenAI could be deployed in ways that compromise safety, privacy, and ethical standards. Establishing robust regulatory frameworks that balance innovation with safety is imperative to harness the benefits of GenAI while mitigating its risks.

The potential for GenAI to be used in cyberattacks is another significant safety concern. Adversarial attacks, where malicious actors manipulate input data to deceive AI systems, can have severe implications. For instance, adversarial examples can cause GenAI models to misclassify data, leading to security breaches or the spread of false information. Enhancing the robustness and security of GenAI systems against such attacks is a critical area of research.

Moreover, the environmental impact of GenAI cannot be overlooked. Training large-scale GenAI models requires substantial computational resources, leading to significant energy consumption and carbon emissions. As the demand for more sophisticated GenAI models grows, so does the environmental footprint. It is crucial to develop more energy-efficient algorithms and explore sustainable practices to mitigate the environmental impact of GenAI.

Finally, the ethical implications of GenAI raise profound safety concerns. The autonomy and decision-making capabilities of GenAI systems pose ethical dilemmas, particularly when these systems are used in sensitive areas such as healthcare, criminal justice, and defense. Ensuring that GenAI systems adhere to ethical principles and human values is essential to prevent harm and maintain public trust.

Addressing these safety concerns requires a multidisciplinary approach, involving collaboration between technologists, ethicists, policymakers, and other stakeholders. By proactively identifying and mitigating the risks associated with GenAI, it is possible to unlock its potential while safeguarding against its dark side.

Impact on Society

The advent of General Artificial Intelligence (GenAI) has brought about transformative changes across various sectors, but it has also cast a long shadow over societal structures. One of the most significant impacts is on employment. The automation of tasks, which were once the domain of human workers, has led to widespread job displacement. Roles in manufacturing, logistics, and even white-collar jobs in finance and healthcare are increasingly being performed by intelligent machines. This shift has created a growing divide between those who possess the skills to work alongside GenAI and those who do not, exacerbating economic inequality.

Another profound effect is on privacy. GenAI systems have the capability to process and analyze vast amounts of personal data with unprecedented accuracy. While this can lead to beneficial outcomes, such as improved healthcare diagnostics and personalized services, it also raises concerns about surveillance and data security. The erosion of privacy is not just a theoretical issue; it has real-world implications for personal freedom and autonomy. Individuals may find themselves subjected to constant monitoring, with their behaviors and preferences meticulously tracked and analyzed.

Social interactions and human relationships are also being reshaped by GenAI. The rise of AI-driven social media algorithms and virtual companions has altered the way people communicate and form connections. These technologies can create echo chambers, where individuals are only exposed to information and viewpoints that reinforce their existing beliefs. This can lead to increased polarization and a fragmented society. Moreover, the reliance on virtual relationships can diminish the quality of face-to-face interactions, potentially leading to feelings of isolation and alienation.

Education systems are undergoing significant changes as well. GenAI offers personalized learning experiences, adapting to the needs and abilities of individual students. While this holds promise for enhancing educational outcomes, it also presents challenges. There is a risk that the overreliance on AI-driven education could de-emphasize the development of critical thinking and creativity, skills that are inherently human. Additionally, access to such advanced educational tools may not be evenly distributed, further entrenching social inequalities.

Healthcare is another domain profoundly affected by GenAI. The ability of AI to analyze medical data and assist in diagnostics has the potential to revolutionize patient care. However, this also raises ethical concerns about the role of human judgment in medical decisions. The depersonalization of healthcare, where patients are treated as data points rather than individuals, could undermine the doctor-patient relationship that is essential for effective care. Moreover, the integration of GenAI in healthcare systems necessitates stringent regulatory frameworks to ensure safety and accountability.

The legal and ethical landscape is struggling to keep pace with the rapid advancements in GenAI. Issues such as accountability, transparency, and bias in AI algorithms are at the forefront of contemporary debates. The potential for AI to perpetuate and even exacerbate existing biases in society is a significant concern. For instance, if a GenAI system is trained on biased data, it may make decisions that unfairly disadvantage certain groups, leading to systemic discrimination.

In sum, while GenAI holds immense potential for societal advancement, it also poses significant challenges that must be addressed. The impact on employment, privacy, social interactions, education, healthcare, and legal frameworks underscores the need for a balanced approach. Society must navigate these complexities with careful consideration to harness the benefits of GenAI while mitigating its darker implications.

Role of Stakeholders

Stakeholders play a significant role in the development, deployment, and governance of General Artificial Intelligence (GenAI). Their influence and actions can shape the trajectory of this powerful technology, determining whether its potential is harnessed for the collective good or leads to detrimental outcomes. Understanding the diverse array of stakeholders and their responsibilities is crucial to navigating the complex landscape of GenAI.

Tech companies are at the forefront of GenAI development. These organizations possess the resources, expertise, and infrastructure necessary to push the boundaries of artificial intelligence. Their decisions on how to design, implement, and market GenAI systems have far-reaching implications. Tech companies must prioritize ethical considerations, transparency, and accountability. By doing so, they can mitigate risks associated with bias, privacy violations, and misuse. Establishing robust ethical guidelines and ensuring compliance through regular audits can help build public trust and foster responsible innovation.

Government bodies and regulatory agencies are tasked with creating a framework that balances innovation with public safety. They must develop comprehensive policies that address the multifaceted challenges posed by GenAI. This includes setting standards for data privacy, algorithmic fairness, and accountability. Governments should engage with a broad spectrum of stakeholders, including academia, industry, and civil society, to ensure that regulations are well-informed and inclusive. Effective oversight mechanisms and adaptive regulatory approaches can help respond to the rapid advancements in GenAI technology.

Academia and research institutions play a pivotal role in advancing the theoretical and practical understanding of GenAI. Researchers contribute to the foundational knowledge that drives technological progress. They also have a responsibility to explore the ethical and societal implications of their work. Collaborative efforts between academic institutions and industry can foster a culture of openness and shared responsibility. By promoting interdisciplinary research and encouraging diverse perspectives, academia can help anticipate and address the broader impacts of GenAI.

Civil society organizations, including non-profits and advocacy groups, serve as watchdogs and advocates for the public interest. They can hold tech companies and governments accountable by highlighting potential risks and advocating for responsible practices. These organizations often represent marginalized communities and can provide valuable insights into the societal impacts of GenAI. By engaging in public discourse, educating the public, and lobbying for ethical standards, civil society groups play a crucial role in ensuring that GenAI development aligns with societal values.

Individuals and end-users are also key stakeholders in the GenAI ecosystem. Their interactions with GenAI systems generate valuable data that fuels further advancements. Users must be informed about the implications of their data usage and have control over their personal information. Public awareness campaigns and education initiatives can empower individuals to make informed decisions and advocate for their rights. Encouraging public participation in policy-making processes can also ensure that diverse voices are heard and considered.

The media has the power to shape public perception and discourse around GenAI. Responsible journalism can provide balanced and accurate information, highlighting both the potential benefits and risks associated with GenAI. By fostering informed discussions and challenging sensationalist narratives, the media can contribute to a more nuanced understanding of the technology.

Each stakeholder group has a unique role to play in the GenAI landscape. Their collective efforts can help navigate the ethical, social, and technical challenges associated with this transformative technology. By fostering collaboration, transparency, and accountability, stakeholders can contribute to a future where GenAI serves the public good and mitigates its darker potential.

Future Directions

The rapid advancement of generative artificial intelligence (GenAI) has already reshaped numerous aspects of society, from creative industries to scientific research. However, the darker implications of these technologies necessitate a careful consideration of future paths. Addressing these concerns involves not only technological innovation but also ethical, legal, and societal frameworks.

One primary area of focus must be the development of robust ethical guidelines and governance structures. The potential for GenAI to create hyper-realistic fake content, manipulate public opinion, or even generate harmful or malicious outputs calls for stringent oversight. Regulatory bodies, in collaboration with tech companies and academic institutions, need to establish clear standards for the responsible use of GenAI. These standards should encompass data privacy, consent, and the transparency of AI-generated content. Furthermore, international cooperation will be essential to create a cohesive global framework that mitigates the risks associated with GenAI.

Another critical direction involves enhancing the transparency and interpretability of GenAI systems. Currently, many GenAI models operate as "black boxes," making it difficult to understand how they arrive at specific outputs. Research into explainable AI (XAI) aims to demystify these processes, providing insights into the decision-making pathways of AI systems. This transparency is crucial not just for building trust among users but also for diagnosing and correcting biases or errors within the models. By prioritizing explainability, developers can create more accountable and reliable systems.

The integration of GenAI into various sectors also necessitates a reevaluation of existing legal frameworks. Intellectual property laws, for instance, are ill-equipped to handle the complexities introduced by AI-generated content. Questions surrounding the ownership and copyright of AI creations require new legal definitions and protections. Additionally, liability issues in cases where AI systems cause harm or produce deceptive content need to be addressed. Legislators and legal experts must work together to update and expand legal doctrines to encompass the unique challenges posed by GenAI.

Education and public awareness are equally important in navigating the future of GenAI. As these technologies become more pervasive, it is crucial for the general public to understand both their capabilities and limitations. Educational initiatives should aim to demystify GenAI, providing individuals with the knowledge to critically evaluate AI-generated content. This can help mitigate the spread of misinformation and empower users to make informed decisions about the technology.

On the technical front, advancing the safety mechanisms within GenAI systems is imperative. Research into adversarial attacks and defenses, for instance, focuses on making AI models more resilient to malicious manipulations. Additionally, the development of robust content moderation tools can help identify and filter harmful or inappropriate AI-generated content. By investing in these safety measures, developers can reduce the potential for misuse and enhance the overall security of GenAI applications.

Collaboration between multidisciplinary fields will also play a significant role in shaping the future of GenAI. Insights from psychology, sociology, and ethics can inform the development of more humane and socially responsible AI systems. Interdisciplinary research can uncover the broader impacts of GenAI on human behavior and societal norms, guiding the creation of technologies that align with collective values and priorities.

In navigating the future of GenAI, a balanced approach that integrates technological innovation with ethical, legal, and societal considerations will be essential. By proactively addressing the potential risks and challenges, we can harness the transformative power of GenAI while safeguarding against its darker implications.

14. Mitigations and Interventions

Mitigation Strategies

The proliferation of Generative Artificial Intelligence (GenAI) has brought about a myriad of benefits, from revolutionizing industries to enhancing everyday tasks. However, its rapid development and deployment have also unveiled several ethical, security, and societal challenges. Addressing these challenges requires a multifaceted approach that encompasses technological, regulatory, and educational strategies.

One core strategy involves the advancement and implementation of robust ethical frameworks. Ethical guidelines should be established to govern the development and use of GenAI. These frameworks must ensure that AI systems are designed with fairness, accountability, and transparency in mind. Developers and organizations should adhere to principles that prevent bias, promote inclusivity, and safeguard user privacy. By embedding ethical considerations into the design process, the risks of unintended consequences can be significantly mitigated.

Regulatory measures play a crucial role in managing the impact of GenAI. Governments and international bodies need to collaborate to create comprehensive regulations that address the unique challenges posed by AI technologies. These regulations should focus on ensuring the safety, security, and reliability of GenAI systems. Establishing standards for AI development and deployment can help prevent misuse and promote responsible innovation. Additionally, regulatory frameworks should include mechanisms for monitoring and enforcing compliance, thereby holding developers and organizations accountable for their actions.

Another vital aspect of mitigating the risks associated with GenAI is enhancing the security of these systems. As AI becomes more integrated into critical infrastructure and decision-making processes, the potential for malicious exploitation increases. Implementing robust cybersecurity measures is essential to protect AI systems from attacks and breaches. This includes employing advanced encryption techniques, conducting regular security audits, and developing AI systems that can detect and respond to threats in real-time. Collaboration between AI developers, cybersecurity experts, and policymakers is necessary to create a secure AI ecosystem.

Education and awareness are fundamental to promoting the responsible use of GenAI. Stakeholders, including developers, policymakers, and the general public, need to be educated about the capabilities and limitations of

AI technologies. This knowledge empowers individuals to make informed decisions and recognize the potential risks associated with AI. Educational initiatives should focus on promoting digital literacy, ethical considerations, and the importance of data privacy. By fostering a culture of awareness and responsibility, society can better navigate the complexities of GenAI.

Interdisciplinary collaboration is essential in addressing the multifaceted challenges of GenAI. Researchers, ethicists, technologists, and policymakers must work together to develop holistic solutions. This collaboration can lead to the creation of interdisciplinary research centers and think tanks dedicated to exploring the ethical, social, and technical dimensions of AI. By bringing together diverse perspectives, these collaborative efforts can generate innovative approaches to mitigate the risks and harness the benefits of GenAI.

Public engagement and participation are also critical in shaping the future of GenAI. Involving the public in discussions about AI policies, ethical considerations, and potential impacts can lead to more inclusive and democratic decision-making processes. Public consultations, forums, and workshops can provide valuable insights and help build trust between AI developers and society. By fostering a participatory approach, stakeholders can ensure that the development and deployment of GenAI align with societal values and priorities.

Mitigating the dark side of GenAI requires a comprehensive and proactive approach that combines ethical considerations, regulatory measures, security enhancements, education, interdisciplinary collaboration, and public engagement. By adopting these strategies, society can navigate the challenges posed by GenAI and harness its potential for the greater good.

Role of Policy Makers

Policy makers play a crucial role in shaping the landscape of generative artificial intelligence (GenAI). Their decisions have far-reaching implications, from establishing ethical guidelines to implementing regulatory frameworks. The rapid advancement of GenAI technologies necessitates a proactive approach to governance, one that balances innovation with societal well-being.

One of the primary responsibilities of policy makers is to ensure that GenAI technologies are developed and deployed ethically. This involves creating guidelines that address issues such as transparency, accountability, and fairness. For instance, policies might mandate that algorithms be explainable, meaning that their decision-making processes can be understood and scrutinized by humans. This is particularly important in high-stakes applications like healthcare or criminal justice, where opaque algorithms could lead to biased or harmful outcomes.

Another critical area for policy intervention is data privacy. GenAI systems often rely on vast amounts of data to function effectively, raising concerns about how this data is collected, stored, and used. Policy makers must establish robust data protection laws that safeguard individuals' privacy while still allowing for the beneficial use of data in training AI models. This could involve regulations that require explicit consent for data use, as well as standards for anonymization and data security.

Intellectual property rights also come into play when discussing GenAI. The ability of these systems to generate content, such as music, art, or text, poses new challenges for copyright law. Policy makers need to consider how to protect the rights of original creators while also fostering an environment that encourages innovation. This might involve creating new categories of intellectual property or adapting existing laws to better fit the unique characteristics of AI-generated content.

The potential for job displacement due to GenAI is another significant concern. While these technologies can enhance productivity and create new types of employment, they can also render certain job categories obsolete. Policy makers must address this issue through labor laws and social safety nets. This could include policies that promote retraining and upskilling programs, ensuring that workers are equipped to transition into new roles created by the AI-driven economy.

Public safety is another domain where policy makers have a vital role. The misuse of GenAI for malicious purposes, such as deepfakes or automated cyber-attacks, poses serious risks. Regulations need to be put in place to prevent and mitigate these threats. This might involve setting standards for the development and deployment of GenAI technologies, as well as creating mechanisms for monitoring and responding to misuse.

International cooperation is essential for effective governance of GenAI. These technologies do not respect national borders, and unilateral policies may be insufficient to address global challenges. Policy makers must therefore engage in international dialogues and treaties to establish common standards and share best practices. This collaborative approach can help harmonize regulations and ensure a more consistent and effective governance framework.

The importance of public engagement cannot be overstated. Policy makers need to involve various stakeholders, including the general public, in the decision-making process. This can be achieved through public consultations, open forums, and transparent communication strategies. By involving a diverse range of voices, policy makers can better understand the societal impacts of GenAI and create policies that are more inclusive and effective.

In summary, policy makers have a multifaceted role in the governance of GenAI. Their actions can shape the ethical, legal, and social dimensions of these technologies, ensuring that they are developed and used in ways that benefit society as a whole.

Role of Researchers

Researchers are at the forefront of advancements in generative artificial intelligence (GenAI), wielding significant influence over its development and application. Their responsibilities extend beyond technical innovation; they are also custodians of ethical standards and societal impacts. The role of researchers in the realm of GenAI is multifaceted, encompassing the creation, refinement, and ethical use of AI technologies.

One primary responsibility of researchers is to advance the technical capabilities of GenAI. This involves developing algorithms, improving machine learning models, and ensuring the systems can generate high-quality, reliable outputs. These technical advancements pave the way for practical applications across various fields, from natural language processing to creative arts and scientific research. Researchers must rigorously test and validate their models to ensure they perform as intended and do not inadvertently produce harmful or biased results.

Ethical considerations are paramount in the development of GenAI. Researchers must navigate complex moral landscapes, balancing innovation with potential societal impacts. This includes addressing issues such as bias, privacy, and the potential for misuse. For instance, a GenAI system trained on biased data could perpetuate or even exacerbate societal inequalities. Researchers are tasked with identifying and mitigating these biases, ensuring their models promote fairness and equity.

Transparency is another crucial aspect of the researchers' role. By openly sharing methodologies, data sources, and findings, researchers contribute to the collective understanding of GenAI and its potential risks and benefits. This transparency fosters a collaborative environment where knowledge is shared and scrutinized, leading to more robust and reliable AI systems. Additionally, transparency helps build public trust in AI technologies, as people are more likely to accept and adopt technologies that are developed openly and responsibly.

Researchers also play a critical role in shaping regulatory frameworks and industry standards. By engaging with policymakers, they can provide valuable insights into the technical and ethical dimensions of GenAI, helping to craft regulations that promote innovation while protecting societal interests. Their expertise ensures that regulations are informed by the latest scientific understanding and technological capabilities, leading to more effective and balanced policies.

The educational role of researchers should not be underestimated. Through academic publications, conferences, and public outreach, they disseminate knowledge and raise awareness about GenAI. This educational effort is vital for cultivating a well-informed public and a new generation of AI researchers who are equipped to tackle future challenges. By fostering a deeper understanding of GenAI, researchers help society prepare for and adapt to the changes brought about by these technologies.

Interdisciplinary collaboration is essential for addressing the multifaceted challenges posed by GenAI. Researchers must work alongside ethicists, sociologists, legal experts, and other stakeholders to ensure a comprehensive approach to AI development. Such collaboration can lead to innovative solutions that consider technical feasibility, ethical implications, and societal needs. This holistic approach is crucial for the responsible advancement of GenAI.

Researchers have a profound responsibility in guiding the trajectory of GenAI. Their work not only drives technological progress but also shapes the ethical and societal landscape in which these technologies operate. By prioritizing transparency, ethical considerations, interdisciplinary collaboration, and public education, researchers can help ensure that GenAI develops in a way that benefits society as a whole. Their role is indispensable in navigating the complexities of this rapidly evolving field, balancing innovation with the imperative to act responsibly and ethically.

Role of Trust and Safety Teams

Trust and Safety Teams are critical in mitigating the risks associated with the deployment of Generative AI technologies. These teams function as the guardians of ethical standards, ensuring that AI systems operate within the boundaries of societal norms and legal frameworks. Their responsibilities encompass a wide range of activities, from policy development and enforcement to user education and incident response.

One of the primary tasks of Trust and Safety Teams is the creation and maintenance of comprehensive guidelines that dictate acceptable use of Generative AI. These guidelines help prevent misuse, such as the generation of harmful or misleading content. Crafting these policies requires a deep understanding of both the technology and its potential societal impacts. It involves collaboration with legal experts, ethicists, and technologists to anticipate and address various risks.

Monitoring and enforcement are crucial components of their role. Trust and Safety Teams employ a mix of automated tools and human oversight to detect and respond to violations of established guidelines. Automated systems can quickly identify patterns indicative of misuse, such as the generation of fake news or deepfakes, but human judgment is often necessary to assess the context and intent behind specific cases. This dual approach ensures a balance between efficiency and accuracy in enforcement actions.

Incident response is another vital aspect of their work. When violations occur, these teams must act swiftly to mitigate harm. This might involve taking down harmful content, notifying affected users, and working with law enforcement if illegal activities are involved. Effective incident response requires robust internal processes and clear communication channels, both within the organization and with external stakeholders.

User education is also a significant responsibility. Trust and Safety Teams develop educational materials and programs to inform users about the ethical use of Generative AI. This includes guidelines on how to recognize and report misuse, as well as best practices for creating content that aligns with community standards. Educating users not only helps prevent misuse but also fosters a culture of responsibility and awareness around AI technologies.

Proactive risk assessment is an ongoing task for these teams. They continuously evaluate emerging threats and vulnerabilities associated with new AI capabilities. This forward-looking approach enables them to update policies and safeguards in anticipation of potential issues, rather than merely reacting to incidents as they arise. It involves staying abreast of advancements in AI research, as well as monitoring trends in malicious activities.

Collaboration is key to the effectiveness of Trust and Safety Teams. They often work closely with other departments, such as product development, legal, and public relations, to ensure a holistic approach to AI governance. This interdisciplinary cooperation helps integrate ethical considerations into the entire lifecycle of AI products, from design and development to deployment and beyond.

The role of Trust and Safety Teams is indispensable in navigating the complexities of Generative AI. By developing robust policies, monitoring compliance, responding to incidents, educating users, assessing risks, and collaborating across functions, these teams help safeguard against the dark side of AI technologies. Their efforts are essential in maintaining the delicate balance between innovation and ethical responsibility, ensuring that the benefits of Generative AI are realized while minimizing potential harms.

Collaborative Efforts

In the rapidly evolving landscape of Generative Artificial Intelligence (GenAI), collaboration has emerged as a critical factor in addressing the multifaceted challenges and opportunities presented by this technology. The development and deployment of GenAI systems involve a diverse array of stakeholders, including researchers, developers, policymakers, ethicists, and end-users. Each group plays a pivotal role in shaping the trajectory of GenAI, ensuring that its benefits are maximized while mitigating potential risks.

One of the primary areas where collaborative efforts are indispensable is in research and development. The complexity of GenAI systems necessitates interdisciplinary collaboration. Computer scientists and engineers work alongside cognitive scientists, linguists, and psychologists to design algorithms that can understand and generate human-like text. This interdisciplinary approach enriches the development process, providing a more comprehensive understanding of the nuances involved in human language and thought processes. Additionally, collaboration with ethicists and sociologists is crucial to embed ethical considerations into the design and functioning of GenAI systems from the outset.

Open-source platforms and collaborative research initiatives have become significant enablers of progress in GenAI. These platforms allow researchers and developers from around the world to share their findings, tools, and datasets, fostering a culture of transparency and collective problem-solving. By pooling resources and knowledge, the GenAI community can tackle complex challenges more efficiently and avoid duplicating efforts. Moreover, open-source collaboration helps in setting industry standards and best practices, which are essential for ensuring the reliability and safety of GenAI applications.

Another critical aspect of collaborative efforts in GenAI is the partnership between the public and private sectors. Governments and regulatory bodies work in tandem with tech companies and research institutions to create policies and frameworks that govern the use of GenAI. These collaborations aim to balance innovation with public interest, ensuring that GenAI technologies are developed responsibly and ethically. Public-private partnerships are also instrumental in funding research and development projects, providing the financial resources necessary to advance the field.

International collaboration is equally important in the realm of GenAI. The global nature of artificial intelligence necessitates cooperation across borders to address issues such as data privacy, security, and the ethical use of AI. International organizations and consortia, such as the Partnership on AI and the Global Partnership on Artificial Intelligence, bring together stakeholders from different countries to discuss and develop guidelines and standards for GenAI. These collaborative efforts are crucial for harmonizing regulations and fostering a global understanding of the implications of GenAI.

User involvement is another vital component of collaborative efforts in GenAI. Engaging end-users in the development process helps ensure that GenAI systems are user-friendly and address real-world needs. Feedback from users provides valuable insights into the practical applications and limitations of GenAI, guiding developers in refining and improving their systems. Moreover, involving diverse user groups in the development process helps in identifying and mitigating biases, ensuring that GenAI systems are inclusive and equitable.

Educational initiatives and public outreach are also essential aspects of collaborative efforts in GenAI. By educating the public and raising awareness about the capabilities and limitations of GenAI, stakeholders can foster a more informed and engaged community. This, in turn, helps in building public trust and acceptance of GenAI technologies.

Collaborative efforts are indispensable in the development and deployment of GenAI. Through interdisciplinary research, open-source platforms, public-private partnerships, international cooperation, user involvement, and educational initiatives, stakeholders can collectively navigate the complexities of GenAI, ensuring that its potential is harnessed responsibly and ethically.

15. Conclusion and Future Outlook

Summary of Key Points

Generative Artificial Intelligence (GenAI) has revolutionized various sectors by automating complex tasks, creating content, and providing advanced analytics. However, it also harbors significant risks and challenges that are often overlooked. This book delves into the darker aspects of GenAI, shedding light on its potential to cause harm if not properly regulated and understood.

One of the primary concerns is the ethical implications of GenAI. As these systems become more sophisticated, the possibility of their misuse increases. Malicious actors can exploit GenAI to create deepfakes, generate misleading information, or even develop autonomous weapons. The ethical quandaries extend to privacy issues as well. With the ability to analyze vast amounts of data, GenAI can potentially infringe on individual privacy, leading to unauthorized surveillance and data breaches.

Another critical point is the bias inherent in GenAI systems. These systems learn from existing data, which often contains historical biases. Consequently, GenAI can perpetuate and even exacerbate these biases, leading to unfair treatment in areas like hiring, law enforcement, and lending. Addressing this issue requires a concerted effort to ensure that training data is as unbiased as possible and that the algorithms are regularly audited for fairness.

The economic impact of GenAI is also a double-edged sword. While it promises increased efficiency and innovation, it also poses a threat to employment. Automation of tasks traditionally performed by humans can lead to significant job displacement. Industries such as manufacturing, customer service, and even creative fields like journalism and art are vulnerable. This shift necessitates a reevaluation of workforce development and education to prepare for an economy increasingly dominated by AI.

Security vulnerabilities are another area of concern. GenAI systems are susceptible to various forms of cyberattacks, including data poisoning, adversarial attacks, and model inversion. These vulnerabilities can compromise the integrity and reliability of the systems, leading to potentially catastrophic outcomes. Ensuring robust security measures and developing resilient AI systems are imperative to mitigate these risks.

The governance and regulation of GenAI present additional challenges. Current regulatory frameworks are often ill-equipped to address the unique issues posed by advanced AI technologies. There is a pressing need for international cooperation to develop comprehensive guidelines and standards that ensure the safe and ethical use of GenAI. Policymakers, technologists, and ethicists must collaborate to create a balanced approach that fosters innovation while protecting society from potential harms.

Lastly, the societal impact of GenAI cannot be ignored. The integration of these systems into everyday life can lead to a range of social issues, including digital divide, loss of human agency, and the erosion of trust in technology. Public awareness and education about the capabilities and limitations of GenAI are crucial in fostering a more informed and cautious approach to its adoption.

Overall, while GenAI holds immense potential for positive impact, it is essential to recognize and address its darker aspects. By understanding the ethical, economic, security, regulatory, and societal challenges, stakeholders can work towards harnessing the benefits of GenAI while minimizing its risks.

Future Trends

The rapid advancement of Generative Artificial Intelligence (GenAI) is reshaping various sectors, creating both opportunities and challenges. As this technology continues to evolve, several trends are likely to emerge, significantly influencing its trajectory and societal impact.

One prominent trend is the increasing sophistication of GenAI models. These models are expected to become more accurate, efficient, and capable of understanding and generating human-like text, images, and even audio. As computational power grows and algorithms become more refined, GenAI systems will be able to produce content that is indistinguishable from that created by humans. This will have profound implications for industries such as entertainment, journalism, and marketing, where the demand for high-quality, customized content is ever-growing.

Another significant trend involves the democratization of GenAI technology. As tools and platforms become more accessible, a wider range of individuals and organizations will be able to harness the power of GenAI. This democratization will spur innovation across various fields, from small businesses leveraging AI to enhance their operations to educational institutions incorporating AI-driven tools into their curriculum. However, this widespread accessibility also raises concerns about misuse and the proliferation of deepfakes, misinformation, and other malicious applications.

The ethical and regulatory landscape surrounding GenAI is also expected to evolve. As the technology becomes more pervasive, there will be a greater emphasis on developing robust frameworks to address ethical considerations and mitigate risks. Policymakers, researchers, and industry leaders will need to collaborate to establish guidelines that ensure the responsible use of GenAI. This includes addressing issues such as bias in AI algorithms, the protection of intellectual property, and the potential for job displacement due to automation.

Privacy concerns will continue to be a critical area of focus. As GenAI systems collect and process vast amounts of data, ensuring the privacy and security of this information will be paramount. Advances in techniques such as federated learning and differential privacy may offer solutions to these challenges by enabling AI models to learn from data without compromising individual privacy. Nonetheless, striking the right balance between innovation and privacy protection will remain a complex and ongoing challenge.

The integration of GenAI with other emerging technologies is another trend that will shape the future landscape. Combining GenAI with advancements in fields such as quantum computing, biotechnology, and the Internet of Things (IoT) could unlock new possibilities and applications. For instance, GenAI-powered IoT devices could revolutionize smart homes and cities, while its integration with biotechnology could lead to breakthroughs in personalized medicine and drug discovery.

The workforce will also experience significant transformations due to the rise of GenAI. While some jobs may become obsolete, new roles and opportunities will emerge, requiring workers to adapt and acquire new skills. Education and training programs will need to evolve to prepare individuals for the changing job market, emphasizing skills such as AI literacy, critical thinking, and creativity.

In the realm of creativity and art, GenAI is poised to become a powerful tool for artists, musicians, and writers. By collaborating with AI, creatives can push the boundaries of their work, exploring new forms of expression and generating innovative ideas. However, this also raises questions about authorship and the value of human creativity in a world where machines can produce art.

As GenAI continues to advance, the interplay between its potential benefits and the associated risks will be a defining feature of its trajectory. By understanding and anticipating these future trends, society can better navigate the complexities and harness the transformative power of GenAI responsibly.

Challenges Ahead

As advancements in Generative Artificial Intelligence (GenAI) continue to accelerate, a variety of challenges emerge that necessitate careful consideration and proactive measures. These challenges span ethical, technical, and societal domains, presenting a complex landscape that stakeholders must navigate to ensure responsible development and deployment of GenAI technologies.

One of the most pressing ethical challenges pertains to the potential for bias in GenAI systems. These systems often learn from vast datasets that may contain historical and societal biases. Consequently, the AI can perpetuate or even amplify these biases, leading to unfair or discriminatory outcomes. For instance, an AI trained on biased data might generate content that disproportionately affects certain demographic groups, thereby reinforcing stereotypes and systemic inequalities. Addressing this issue requires rigorous oversight, diverse training datasets, and continuous monitoring to mitigate bias and ensure fairness.

Privacy concerns also loom large in the realm of GenAI. As these systems become more sophisticated, they increasingly rely on personal data to generate accurate and contextually relevant outputs. However, the collection and use of such data raise significant privacy issues. Unauthorized access, data breaches, and misuse of personal information are risks that need robust safeguards. Implementing stringent data protection measures and ensuring transparency in data usage are critical steps in protecting individual privacy.

The technical challenges associated with GenAI are equally formidable. One major issue is the interpretability of these systems. GenAI models, particularly deep learning networks, often function as "black boxes," making it difficult to understand how they arrive at specific decisions or outputs. This lack of transparency can hinder trust and accountability, especially in high-stakes applications such as healthcare or criminal justice. Researchers are actively exploring methods to enhance the interpretability of AI models, but achieving a balance between complexity and comprehensibility remains a significant hurdle.

Scalability is another technical challenge. As GenAI models grow in size and complexity, their computational demands increase exponentially. This poses significant constraints on resources, including processing power and energy consumption. Efficient algorithms and hardware optimizations are essential to manage these demands and ensure that GenAI systems can scale effectively without unsustainable resource usage.

On a societal level, the integration of GenAI into various sectors raises questions about job displacement and economic inequality. Automation driven by GenAI has the potential to replace human labor in numerous fields, from manufacturing to creative industries. While this could lead to increased efficiency and productivity, it also risks exacerbating unemployment and widening the gap between those who can adapt to new technological paradigms and those who cannot. Policymakers and industry leaders must collaborate to create strategies that support workforce transition, such as reskilling programs and social safety nets.

Moreover, the rapid development of GenAI technologies necessitates robust regulatory frameworks. Existing laws and regulations often lag behind technological advancements, creating a regulatory void that can be exploited. Establishing clear guidelines and standards for the ethical use of GenAI is imperative to prevent misuse and ensure that these technologies are developed and deployed in a manner that aligns with societal values and norms.

Addressing these multifaceted challenges requires a concerted effort from researchers, developers, policymakers, and the public. By fostering interdisciplinary collaboration and maintaining a vigilant approach to ethical, technical, and societal implications, the potential of GenAI can be harnessed responsibly, paving the way for innovations that benefit humanity as a whole.

Opportunities for Positive Use

While the potential pitfalls and ethical dilemmas surrounding General Artificial Intelligence (GenAI) are significant, it is equally important to highlight the opportunities for positive use. GenAI, when harnessed responsibly, can offer transformative benefits across various sectors, from healthcare to education, environmental conservation, and beyond. The key to unlocking these benefits lies in a judicious blend of innovation, regulation, and ethical considerations.

One of the most promising applications of GenAI is in the field of healthcare. Advanced AI systems can analyze vast datasets to identify patterns that might elude human experts. For instance, GenAI can assist in early diagnosis of diseases by recognizing subtle indicators in medical imaging, genetic data, or patient histories. This capability not only enhances the accuracy of diagnoses but also enables personalized treatment plans tailored to individual patients' needs. Furthermore, AI-driven drug discovery processes can significantly accelerate the development of new medications, potentially leading to breakthroughs in treating complex diseases.

In the realm of education, GenAI can revolutionize the way knowledge is imparted and acquired. Personalized learning platforms powered by AI algorithms can adapt to the unique learning styles and paces of individual students. This customization can help bridge educational gaps and foster a more inclusive learning environment, ensuring that all students have the opportunity to reach their full potential. Additionally, AI can assist educators by automating administrative tasks, allowing them more time to focus on teaching and mentoring students.

Environmental conservation is another area where GenAI can make a substantial impact. AI systems can monitor environmental changes in real-time, providing valuable data for conservation efforts. For example, AI-powered drones can track wildlife populations, monitor deforestation, and detect illegal poaching activities. By analyzing this data, conservationists can develop more effective strategies to protect endangered species and preserve natural habitats. Moreover, AI can optimize resource management in agriculture, reducing waste and promoting sustainable farming practices.

The business sector also stands to gain from the positive use of GenAI. AI-driven analytics can provide companies with deeper insights into market trends, consumer behavior, and operational efficiencies. This information can inform strategic decisions, leading to more innovative products and services. Additionally, AI can enhance customer experiences through personalized interactions, improving satisfaction and loyalty. In the manufacturing industry, AI can optimize supply chains, predict maintenance needs, and enhance quality control, ultimately boosting productivity and reducing costs.

However, the realization of these positive outcomes is contingent upon addressing the ethical challenges associated with GenAI. Ensuring transparency, accountability, and fairness in AI systems is paramount. Developing robust frameworks for data privacy and security is essential to protect individuals' rights and maintain public trust. Collaboration between governments, academia, industry, and civil society is crucial to establish guidelines and standards that promote the responsible use of AI.

Moreover, fostering a culture of ethical AI development involves continuous education and awareness. Stakeholders must stay informed about the evolving landscape of AI technologies and their implications. Encouraging interdisciplinary research can also provide diverse perspectives on the ethical and societal impacts of GenAI, leading to more holistic and inclusive solutions.

In conclusion, while the dark side of GenAI cannot be ignored, its potential for positive use offers a compelling counterbalance. By navigating the ethical complexities and harnessing the power of AI responsibly, society can unlock unprecedented opportunities for advancement and well-being. The challenge lies in striking the right balance between innovation and regulation, ensuring that the benefits of GenAI are realized while mitigating its risks.

Final Thoughts

The rapid advancement of Generative AI (GenAI) technologies has brought about a profound transformation in numerous sectors, from healthcare and education to entertainment and finance. However, as with any powerful tool, the potential benefits are accompanied by significant risks and ethical considerations. Throughout this book, we have explored the multifaceted nature of GenAI, delving into its capabilities, applications, and the darker aspects that warrant careful scrutiny.

One of the primary concerns surrounding GenAI is the potential for misuse. The ability of these systems to generate highly realistic text, images, and even videos opens up avenues for deception and misinformation at an unprecedented scale. Deepfakes, for instance, can be used to create convincing but entirely fabricated content, posing threats to personal privacy, political stability, and public trust. The challenge lies in developing robust detection mechanisms and establishing legal frameworks to mitigate these risks without stifacing innovation.

Another critical issue is the ethical dimension of GenAI. The deployment of these technologies often involves complex decisions about bias, fairness, and accountability. As GenAI systems are trained on vast datasets, they can inadvertently perpetuate or even amplify existing biases present in the data. This raises questions about the fairness of AI-driven decisions in areas such as hiring, law enforcement, and lending. It is imperative for developers and policymakers to prioritize transparency and inclusivity, ensuring that GenAI systems serve all segments of society equitably.

Privacy concerns also loom large in the discourse on GenAI. The data required to train these systems is often vast and personal, encompassing everything from social media activity to medical records. Safeguarding this data against breaches and ensuring that it is used responsibly is paramount. The implementation of stringent data protection measures and adherence to privacy regulations can help in addressing these concerns, but the evolving nature of technology necessitates continuous vigilance and adaptation.

In addition to these ethical and societal issues, the economic implications of GenAI cannot be ignored. While automation and enhanced productivity promise significant economic benefits, they also pose challenges to the labor market. Jobs that involve repetitive tasks or basic decision-making are particularly vulnerable to automation, leading to potential displacement of workers. It is crucial to invest in education and reskilling programs to prepare the workforce for the changing landscape and to explore policies that support a just transition.

The environmental impact of GenAI is another area that demands attention. Training large-scale AI models is an energy-intensive process, contributing to the carbon footprint. As concerns about climate change intensify, it is essential to develop more energy-efficient algorithms and explore sustainable practices in AI research and deployment.

The future of GenAI is undeniably promising, with the potential to revolutionize industries and improve quality of life. However, realizing this potential requires a balanced approach that acknowledges and addresses the associated risks. Collaboration among technologists, ethicists, policymakers, and the public is crucial in navigating the complex terrain of GenAI. By fostering an environment of responsible innovation, it is possible to harness the transformative power of GenAI while safeguarding against its darker facets.

As we move forward, continuous dialogue and proactive measures will be essential in shaping a future where GenAI contributes positively to society. The insights and discussions presented in this book aim to provide a foundation for such efforts, encouraging a thoughtful and informed approach to the development and deployment of Generative AI technologies.

ABOUT THE AUTHOR

Dr. Ivan Del Valle is an International Business Transformation Executive with extensive senior leadership experience in strategy and management consulting at top firms like Accenture and Capgemini. He led the data integration for one of the largest touchless planning and fulfillment implementations in the world for a $346 billion healthcare company. Born and raised on the picturesque Caribbean island of Puerto Rico, he currently resides with his beloved wife and Cavalier King Charles Spaniels in the historic district of Charleston, South Carolina, in the United States.

He earned a Ph.D. in Law from Apsley Business School in London, UK, focusing his research on the laws and regulations pertaining to the legal aspects of blockchain-driven international trade traceability in sustainable food chains. On his current role as a Global Enterprise Data & Analytics Executive at Boston Scientific, he spearheads a broad range of initiatives across Data Engineering and Machine Learning/AI. His proficiency pioneering the development of Generative AI use cases within the Medical Devices sector as an integral part of the Life Sciences industry is internationally recognized. His leadership in these innovative areas underscores a commitment to advancing data analytics and AI applications in healthcare technology.

In addition to his hands-on, value driven credentials, Dr. Del Valle holds an MBA from the University of The People in Pasadena, California, a Master's in Data Science & Analytics from the prestigious Nebrija University in Madrid, Spain, and a Master's degree in Consumer Neuroscience (Neuromarketing) from UNIR Mexico. He lectures at Apsley Business School London, covering Applied AI Advanced topics, International & Comparative Law, Strategic Management and Organizational Theory, and is a regular panel participant in leading-edge, international, multi-industry conferences.

Dr. Del Valle can be reached via LinkedIn at
https://www.linkedin.com/in/enterprise-solutions

The Dark Side of GenAI - Exploitation and Compromise of GenAI Systems and Capabilities

www.ingramcontent.com/pod-product-compliance
Lightning Source LLC
Chambersburg PA
CBHW031622210526
45464CB00004B/1707